Wicked TAOS

Ellen Dornan

I0809739

The History PRESS

Published by The History Press
Charleston, SC 29403
www.historypress.net

Copyright © 2014 by Ellen Dornan
All rights reserved

First published 2014

Manufactured in the United States

ISBN 978.1.62619.307.9

Library of Congress CIP data applied for.

Notice: The information in this book is accurate and complete to the best of our knowledge. It is offered without guarantee on the part of the author or The History Press. The author and The History Press disclaim all liability in connection with the use of this book.

All rights reserved. No part of this book may be reproduced or transmitted in any form whatsoever without prior written permission from the publisher except in the case of brief quotations embodied in critical articles and reviews.

CONTENTS

PREFACE

The Taos Valley remains largely rural, encompassing a scattering of separate communities, including Taos Pueblo, Ranchos de Taos, the town of Taos (still known to some as Don Fernando de Taos) and numerous tiny villages. The towering Sangre de Cristo Mountains, beloved by Taos artists, shelter more traditional villages. Because the Rio Grande scores a deep gorge through the plateau to the west, the topography has always encouraged commerce to the east, where the Great Plains commence beyond the mountains.

The ancient highway from Santa Fe to Taos is finally paved, but the narrow, twisty road is lined with *descansos*—roadside crosses—that remind the traveler of the perils inherent in a visit to the magnificent valley and its surrounding peaks. On the face of it, the culture in Taos is not so different from that of Santa Fe or Albuquerque, yet Taos retains a mystique—and perhaps an air of danger—that has vanished from other New Mexican communities.

Any historian or political observer can note more wickedness in a month in the streets of Albuquerque or in the halls of Santa Fe's Roundhouse than happens in a generation in the quiet villages of the Taos Valley. We should feel fortunate because when the Taos get angry enough to leave their fields and pastures, few survivors remain to tell the tale.

These village folk have sparked every revolution that toppled a New Mexican government, whether Spanish, Mexican or American. Making war might not be wicked in itself, but the Taos uprisings are characterized by widespread slaughter of noncombatants and the utter destruction of churches, homes and businesses. In any of these wars, there was plenty of wicked behavior on both sides. Are the oppressed rebels or the cruel oppressors to blame for a bloody revolution? When men take up arms to defend their way of life, does that make them murderers or heroes?

Culturally, the peaceful residents of the Taos Valley are hardly wicked but rather radical in ways that might have seemed wicked to past generations. There is no indication that this community of pious Catholics ever supported a brothel, but the community showed broad tolerance toward both openly gay and interracial couples long before the rest of the country followed suit.

Some historical wickedness seems mild to jaded twenty-first-century sensibilities. Blasphemy, heresy, adultery, sodomy and miscegenation are no longer crimes or even particularly offensive to most minds (unless, perhaps, it's your daughter involved). Peyote and marijuana now have quasi-legal status in New Mexico and elsewhere in the nation.

However, many of Taos's blackest moments and shadiest characters can't be painted as anything but terribly wicked; slaughtering children, trafficking in drugs or slaves, violent oppression, stealing from the poor, rape and the use of black magic still qualify.

New Mexico has a sadly incomplete documentary history, and Taos is no exception. Myths and legends, recounted during long winter evenings, make up most of what we know of life in Taos during the centuries before the arrival of the Europeans. Records were destroyed or never created in the first place. Taos barely appeared on maps until the nineteenth century, and local doings rarely came to the attention of authorities. Oral history recollections, while juicier than the official record, often contain conflicting, misremembered and even invented information. I have tried to pursue a middle path, combining the facts as recorded in official records and stories recounted by witnesses, elders and town gossips.

I am grateful to The History Press for the opportunity to learn more about the history of this fascinating place. Thanks so much to my polymath partner, Craig Goldsmith, who has supported this work with editorial expertise, patience and love; and to the brilliant, witty and utterly inimitable historian Ramona Caplan, for diligently fact checking my writing.

Special thanks to talented artist Jane Abrams, as well as Clinton and Jane Anderson of Taos and the University of New Mexico's Center for Southwest Research. Together, they graciously granted permission to publish Ms. Abrams's spectacular prints from Willard "Spud" Johnson's collection of wood blocks. These blocks were carved by a number of Taos artists in

A busy day on Taos Plaza. Jane Abrams print. *University of New Mexico Center for Southwest Research (CSWR).*

the early twentieth century as illustrations for Johnson's print publications, *Laughing Horse* and the *Horse Fly* (the "smallest and most inadequate newspaper ever published"), which later became a column in the newspaper *El Crepúsculo*. I have made every possible effort to verify copyright for the images reproduced in this book; the other photos and images are used by permission of the artist or copyright holder or under a Creative Commons license, except those that have entered the public domain.

I

TRADITIONAL TROUBLEMAKERS

Archaeologists estimate that the first settlers in the Taos Valley built their first settlement—of pit houses—between 1100 and 1200 CE. Over subsequent centuries, the people of the valley gradually improved and expanded their dwellings, creating the monumental adobe structures that now characterize the pueblo. The earliest descriptions of the pueblo, straddling the river that flows from the sacred Blue Lake up in the Sangre de Cristo Mountains, still ring true to modern visitors. The Taos and nearby Picuris are the only Tiwa who lived in the north and in some ways shared more with the neighboring Jicarilla Apache than with the southern Tiwa. All these tribes agree that wickedness was a serious problem before people even came into this world.

Wickedness Before the World Began

Legends tell us that before this world, there was another—the Third World. The Third World was a lovely place, but the people became quarrelsome. They gave in to their lustful urges and copulated indiscriminately. Children defied and disobeyed their parents and even fought one another. The people ignored the divine plan and pursued their own pleasure without thought for the consequences. As a result of this misbehavior, the world was destroyed. A small group of survivors clustered on top of a mountain until a holy spirit guided them to the new world.

Although these survivors included the most obedient of the people of the Third World, there were some promiscuous women who were pregnant from their frenzied fornication. These women managed to survive the long journey to the Fourth World, only to give birth to monsters on their arrival. These monsters were a great misery to the early people of Taos and included a race of giants, as well as a tribe of vicious, bloodthirsty redheads.

While some believe that the place of emergence was Blue Lake, the Jicarilla say that the original lake has now dried. The place of emergence has been burned over twice by fire, and if it burns again, the "fire is going to start there and burn all over the world." This will happen when the people who emerged become few in number, and the Fourth World will be destroyed just as the other worlds before it.

The First Conflicts

When the people first emerged into the Fourth World, many left the area and created other tribes. The Taos people wandered for a bit and then returned to their place of emergence. Modern storytellers refer to this period as "when we lived in the forest" and the "time of the cottonwoods."

The people presumably remembered that their fractious behavior had caused the destruction of their entire previous world, but old habits are hard to break. When the Summer People were finished wandering the lands to the south, they returned to find the Winter People had migrated down from the mountain to their current location on the river. Receiving a hostile reception from the Winter People, the Summer People sent an envoy to negotiate.

"What do you have to say? Are you friends or enemies?" demanded the envoy.

"We are not your friends," replied the Winter People's representative.

"It is well. We will fight you," the man from the Summer People answered, and he returned to his camp to prepare for war. The Winter People barricaded themselves into their kivas, but the Summer People poured "medicine" into the holes, which drove the Winter People out. Cowed by the superior strength of the Summer People's power, the Winter People abjectly surrendered. The chief of the Summer People told the Winter People that he was their father and they were his children. He adopted them all into the clan, and from that point onward, they shared government and ceremonial duties and lived in harmony. (Much later, the Water People swam to Taos in the form of fish, but that is a story for another time.)

Rock art near Taos in the Rio Grande del Norte National Monument. *Courtesy Bureau of Land Management, New Mexico State Office.*

The people had made peace with one another, but a terrible monster called Holds in the Water endangered them all. As the Jicarilla tell it, the people should have fought or at least run away from the monsters in those early days, but they were living as if in a dream. They simply accepted the possibility of attack while growing corn, hunting and even gathering water. Holds in the Water was notorious for drowning maidens who came to fill their water jars and would pull any unsuspecting person under the waves. Even as the heroic twins born to the Sun and White-Painted Woman killed off monster after monster elsewhere in New Mexico, Holds in the Water drowned people unmolested. In fact, the older he became, the crankier he became.

THE LAST MONSTER

The most active twin, Killer of Enemies, had gotten old, too, and perhaps a bit curmudgeonly. He was spending his golden years traveling around to the pueblos, teaching them the arts of war. For some time, he had been teaching the Picurís everything he knew, making them terribly fierce. He rewarded his students with the skill of making eagle feather war bonnets. But even a long and pleasant visit has to end. Since he was close by, Killer of Enemies turned toward Taos.

The Taos people found the old man repulsive. "Get away, you raggedy Apache," they jeered, and drove him off. He snuck back and hid in a kiva while the men were doing their work. They did not see him at first, but when all their corn turned into nasty black flies, they searched for the culprit and tossed him out a second time.

Again and again, Killer of Enemies snuck into the kiva to punish the men who had ill-treated him. One time, he turned the corn to slimy, wriggling worms. Another time, he caused all the men's heads to stick together. Each time, the people would beg and plead for charity and forgiveness, but when Killer of Enemies waved his hand and returned things to normal, they forgot their promises and threw him out again. Finally, they realized that the raggedy, dirty old man they were shunning was really the powerful and legendary monster slayer and the answer to their prayers.

Now the people came to Killer of Enemies and begged him to put an end to Holds in the Water. They tearfully described the lost girls and the fear all the people suffered. Killer of Enemies demanded a complete suit of armor made entirely of turquoise. At first, the Taos people tried decorating him with some choice bangles, but when they realized he was serious, they decked him out from head to toe in fabulous overlapping turquoise plates.

Protected in this way, he walked to the lake and drained it with his magic. In the empty lake, a ladder led down below the algae. Killer of Enemies descended the ladder and found Holds in the Water sitting naked at the bottom. Taking advantage of the unaccustomed sunshine, the terrible monster had spread out all his clothes and was cracking the lice as they emerged.

The monster's wife came running out, scolding her husband. "Put your clothes on, old man!" she screeched. "We have company."

Holds in the Water got dressed and greeted his guest politely, but Killer of Enemies did not keep the conversation friendly for long. He accused Holds in the Water of dragging people under the water and holding them forever. The couple strenuously denied the accusations. Killer of Enemies demanded the return of the monsters' captives. Again, the couple denied having a single captive. Killer of Enemies made a fire, filling the house with bitter smoke. The couple choked on the smoke and relented, releasing a handful of captives. He asked the monsters if these were the only captives, and they swore this was the case while coughing painfully. Killer of Enemies made more smoke in the house, and before long, the gasping couple released another group of captives. Over the monsters' denials, Killer of Enemies persisted until he had smoked out every last captive.

Freed, the drowned people all returned to their families with much rejoicing. Killer of Enemies still had the problem of the lake monsters. He could kill them, but he was tired of killing monsters. Deciding that they were much too powerful together, he split them up, sending them to live in separate lakes near what is now Alamosa, Colorado. Holds in the Water and his wife were furious at being separated and swore eternal vengeance against humans. They each vowed to drown every person who entered the waters of their lakes, with no exceptions. Killer of Enemies answered, "So be it," and banished the two from Taos forever.

These were the last monsters to live in Taos. Killer of Enemies left not long after that, allowing people to create their own ways in the world. Unfortunately, some people had been contaminated by the monsters and turned to sorcery and other evil ways. Their contagion could easily infect others, and witches could enchant even otherwise good people to do wicked deeds. This was certainly the case for many a straying husband (and a few wives), who consistently attributed their infidelity to the effects of witchcraft.

Taos witches caused the same kinds of unpleasantness as witches elsewhere, such as spreading death and destruction to livestock, crops and children. Rather than flying on brooms, the Taos witches traveled in the skin of animals. When they needed to fly, they took the form of owls or other birds of prey. Witches remained a misery to the Puebloans and Spanish of Taos for centuries.

All the witches lived in a place called *Uwaalaka*. At night (and sometimes even during the day), the witches took the form of animals and traveled to secret caves in the canyons to meet with others of their kind. At these meetings, witches plotted their schemes. If they wanted to put a spell on someone, they blew enchanted rocks, shards and other projectiles into the person's body. Although these projectiles left no visible mark, they would sicken the victim, putting him or her under the power of the sorcerers. Only a powerful healer could remove the witch stones.

A Plague of Witches

In the time of the cottonwood, there was a man who had two beautiful wives, Blue Corn Maiden and Yellow Corn Maiden. These women both fell under the spell of some terrible witches. The witches caused them to be unfaithful to their husband and to become promiscuous and lying.

The stories about what happened next differ, but in no version of the tale do things turn out well for the wives. Their husband followed them to *Uwaalaka* and saw them copulating with the witches (who were mostly male). In some stories, the husband killed one wife, and the other wife decided to be faithful to him. In other stories, he killed both wives.

Witches didn't leave the Taos girls alone, either. A witch boy had his eye on a certain pretty girl, but she refused him, so he killed her. The witches stole her body and then used magic to pull the bewitched arrows, spikes and stones out of her body while laughingly comparing their skills at sorcery. The girl's little sister witnessed the theft of the corpse and followed the witches. She watched from behind a rock in mounting horror. The witches revived her dead sister only to turn her into a deer so they could hunt her and kill her again. As the witches rained arrows down on the terrified doe, the little sister ran home, appalled, helpless to stop the evil acts.

In the morning, a neighbor woman stopped by the girl's house with a basket of fresh venison. The sister bravely drove the woman away, shouting, "We don't eat people! Only witches eat people! You eat it yourself, you cannibal!" Heeding the girl's cries, the people of the Pueblo drove the woman and the other witches out.

In revenge, the witches caused many people to sicken and even die. The witches had discovered a way to make themselves invisible so hunters could not find them. Finally, the Taos people trekked up to where Deer Woman lived in the mountains and asked her for help. She suggested that the witches could not resist a bet. If her two strong and fleet sons ran against the witches, they would surely prevail, and then the witches would have to leave.

As predicted, the witches agreed to the bet but insisted the race be around the whole world. When the Deer Woman's sons showed up, the people's hearts sank. The boys were nothing but skeletons with a little flesh. How could these skinny boys possibly outrun witches? The old men decided that all they could do was pray for victory.

The witches turned themselves into falcons, and soon they flew ahead of the Deer Boys, laughing and taunting them. The boys had been expecting this and took out little bags of medicine that they used to create a brutal thunderstorm. The thunder frightened the witch falcons, the rain soaked them and the lightning finally drove them to seek shelter. The birds huddled under a tree miserably, but the Deer Boys didn't mind the wet and bounded ahead.

Race to Taos Pueblo. Jane Abrams print of Ila McAfee's carving for "The Horse Fly" section of the Taos newspaper *El Crepúsculo*, September 1950. *CSWR*.

By the time the witches' feathers were dry enough to fly, the Deer Boys were almost all the way around the world. The witch falcons doubled their speed until they could see the boys and flew even faster. The people and the witches were waiting at the finish line with their clubs, each waiting for their team to cross the finish line before killing the others. The Deer Boys finished just ahead of the witches, and the people fell on the witches with their clubs before the falcons could even cross the line themselves. The people killed all the witches except one, an old man.

He fell on his knees and pleaded for mercy, promising to change his ways and do only good for the rest of his days. Many disbelieved the words of the witch and were in favor of killing him. Some kindhearted souls argued that he was an old man and could do little harm. In the end, mercy won the day, and the old man was allowed to leave. Treacherously, he did not give up his evil ways, and today all witches on the earth are descended from the one witch allowed to survive.

Eventually, people learned effective ways of catching witches. The most common method entailed killing and skinning all stray animals. One night at Taos Junction, a man killed a witch in this way. While he was riding home, a huge black dog came bounding out of the brush and menaced him. He drew his bow and shot the dog with arrows until it fell dead. Cautiously, he used a knife to skin the dog and discovered a man curled up inside the dog skin. The Taos man recognized the dead *brujo* as one of a group of witches from Santo Domingo and Tesuque.

Another innovative Taos technique for capturing witches was making a "Juan circle." First, a big circle is drawn. Then, a man named Juan enters the circle and turns his shirt inside out. The witches are irresistibly drawn into the circle and can be easily killed. Two men from Taos named Juan made quite a name for themselves as witch hunters and caught dozens of witches with this method.

COYOTE CAUSES TROUBLE

Both the people of Taos Pueblo and the Jicarilla Apache tell stories about Coyote. Coyote not only brought the buffalo to Taos, but he also taught the Taos people the buffalo dance. Although he was a powerful being, Coyote needed no witchcraft to get into all kinds of trouble. His greed drove him all over the world. He was always after other people's food or talents, even if they were not appropriate for a Coyote. Because he was too lazy to work for what he wanted, he caused terrible problems for himself and others.

Because he was always driven from place to place, Coyote became lazy about where he did his business and often relieved himself right in the middle of the road. This was particularly dangerous because witches commonly enchanted urine-soaked mud balls and rolled the hexed mud toward women to make them have twins. Coyote's filthy habits not only got him in trouble, but they also ended a golden era for the people of Taos.

When the people still lived in the forest, there were two kind, friendly boulders that loved humans. When the people traveled around the world, the giant rocks went with them. The boulders hunted buffalo and deer by rolling over the game animals' legs. They protected the people from harm. When anyone from Taos felt a need, he petitioned the rocks, and the rocks would deliver the request in the twinkling of an eye. In this way, the rocks made life easy and peaceful for everyone.

Coyote, the primeval trickster of the Southwest.

But Coyote wanted some fun with the rocks himself. He ran over to the rocks and began bounding from one to the other and running around them in circles. The rocks were annoyed. "Coyote, stop. You are acting very foolish!"

"Pretty rocks! Nice rocks! Why shouldn't I run around you?" Coyote asked insolently.

"Coyote, get away now! You are too ignorant!" the boulders commanded.

Coyote was mad about being called foolish and ignorant. Deciding to teach the rocks a lesson, he jumped on top of the boulders and pooped down their sides. The rocks were furious and started to roll after Coyote. Alarmed, he ran around the world, begging the rocks to give up the chase. The rocks persisted until they had chased Coyote all the way back to Taos. There, they flattened him, rolled to a stop and rested. They would not help the people anymore; nor would they move. Eventually, the rocks fused together, but you can still see the smear that Coyote left.

After Coyote recovered from being flattened, he began feeling awfully guilty about his misdeed. He decided to go far away, where people wouldn't know about his mischief, and started traveling down the road again. Soon he smelled food and sniffed out a little sleeping mouse named *Paukauuna*. Coyote's snuffling woke the mouse, which was afraid but determined not to become dinner. Coyote smiled toothily at Paukauuna.

"You are so fat and pretty, Grandson," he greeted the mouse.

Paukauuna pretended to be annoyed and hissed at Coyote. "Shhh, Grandfather, I'm trying to listen to the people down below. They are talking, and it may be important." The little rodent laid one of his big ears flat to the ground and pretended he was following a conversation.

Predictably, Coyote became wildly curious. He put his ear to the ground but could hear nothing. "Eh? What is it? I can't hear! What are they saying?"

Solemnly, Paukauuna told him, "The people down below say that anyone who has been urinating or defecating in the road or on top of stones, anywhere in the world, is sure to die a horrible death."

Coyote jumped up. "Oh, it is too much!" he wailed. "You must not ever tell, but a little while ago, I urinated and defecated on some rocks. Please don't tell the people down below!"

With that, he ran away at top speed. Paukauuna laughed and said, "Any little thing will scare Coyote. Now he will never come back, and I will live in peace." And he did.

However, Coyote was far from done with his tricks. While watching the Apache maidens gather water from a lake, he had a clever idea. He took white mud and painted himself all over with it. He found some feathers and stuck them in his muddy fur, then hid himself in the center of the lake.

Before long, two Jicarilla maidens came down to the lake to get water. Coyote rose up, roaring at the terrified girls. "I am *Pakothlanana*, Big Water Man!" he shouted. "Wade in deeper, but lift your skirts up so you don't get wet!"

The trembling girls did as he said.

"Keep going!" he commanded.

The girls took a step forward.

"Don't get your skirts wet! Lift them up!" he barked. Gradually, he lured them into the water until they were waist deep.

During this time, the other girls noticed their friends had been gone a long time. When they arrived at the lake, Coyote pulled the same trick on them. More girls came down to the lake, looking for their friends, and soon every girl in the tribe was standing waist deep in the water, fearfully holding her skirt high. Coyote leapt out of the water and ran into their encampment, shouting, "All the Apache women are mine! I know them all!" The Taos people say that every girl returned home pregnant.

As the Apaches learned, to their sorrow, Coyote was wicked when it came to women. In truth, he was just as lustful as he was greedy. One time, he pretended to be Old Man Gopher and raped Old Woman Gopher. When Old Woman Gopher demanded revenge for her injury, Old Man Gopher replied that he was too small and afraid. Coyote even tricked his own daughter into marrying him. Coyote girls must be gutsier than gopher men because she stabbed her father to death when she discovered the deception.

PEDRO ORDIMALAS

The Spanish settlers of Taos left almost nothing in the way of written history but have perpetuated a rich oral tradition. Many generations of storytellers have embellished on the story of Pedro Ordimalas, a notorious man-child who nonetheless ended up in Paradise.

Both the Spanish settlers and the Pueblo people had an abhorrence of useless, lazy people, and Pedro Ordimalas was such a wastrel that no one wanted him around. Even his family gave him a hard time for his gambling and bad habits. He didn't mind, though; he could find company down at the cantina any day or night as long as he could swindle someone out of enough money to join a card game.

Two merchants that Pedro Ordimalas tricked decided that the world would be better off without such a layabout. They found Pedro snoozing under a shady cottonwood and, quick as a wink, bundled him into a sack and started to haul him down to the river. But the river was far, the trail was steep and the sun was hot. The two merchants were irritable when they got down to the river, and discovering how shallow it was just made them angrier. They began to fight about where the closest deep water might be found and ended up going their separate ways up the river, leaving the heavy Pedro tied in his sack.

As he lay there, a shepherd boy happened along and spotted the sack. He poked at it cautiously. Pedro began to sob and wail. "Don't make me go, you horrible man! I don't want to be the *alcalde mayor*! I don't want all that money. Please don't make me move into that big *hacienda* or marry your daughter!"

Intrigued, the shepherd asked him to calm down and tell his story. Sniffling, Pedro answered that some men wanted him to become the alcalde of Taos, and although they were willing to pay him hundreds of *pesos* and house him in a spacious hacienda, Pedro still refused. The men offered him their beautiful daughters in marriage, but he remained firm, so the men abducted him. "And so," sighed Pedro, "here I am, on my way to a life of riches and luxury, but I would rather be a simple shepherd."

Moved by Pedro's tale, the shepherd boy immediately thought of a solution and offered to trade places with Pedro. He untied the bag, released Pedro and had Pedro tie the sack up. Pedro drove the sheep away gleefully and left the poor boy to his fate. Pedro sold the sheep immediately, but rather than give the money to his poor wife and hungry children, he played cards until the last coin was gone.

He set out to find work and soon met a rich farmer who needed a reliable helper. The farmer offered ten pesos in advance if Pedro would sign on for a year of service. Pedro eagerly accepted the money and agreed to the terms, but he was much too lazy to do any of the work that needed doing. The farmer sent Pedro out to weed the wheat fields, but Pedro thought it would be faster to burn the weeds—and it was too bad if the wheat burned, too.

The farmer wanted to fire Pedro on the spot, but Pedro reminded him of the contract. Thinking Pedro would learn some humility among the women, the exasperated farmer sent Pedro to tend to his spoiled son. Right off, the child threw a mighty tantrum when Pedro would not give him some treat he desired. Pedro grabbed the boy and spanked him until his mother came running in.

She begged Pedro to stop, but he refused, claiming that he would answer only to his employer, her husband. The child's wails drove the mother to find the farmer and insist that Pedro be sent away. The farmer ordered Pedro to go, begged Pedro to go and, finally, paid Pedro a hefty reward to leave.

Pedro took the money straight to the gambling *sala* and involved himself in a card game. But even the fat bag of coins the rich farmer had paid him didn't last long, and soon he was reduced to watching the card game and cadging drinks from friends.

Some beggars came in looking for charity. All the card players jeered at them, punched them and drove them back out, but Pedro felt unaccustomedly guilty. He swiped a few coins off the card table and ran after the beggars, pressing the money on them.

As it turned out, the "beggars" were really Jesus and St. Peter, and they were so grateful for the charity that they offered Pedro Ordimalas anything he wanted. He asked for—and received—a magical pack of playing cards that would always give him winning hands and a drum that forces the player to keep playing and playing and playing. After fulfilling these strange requests, Jesus urged Pedro to ask for one more thing.

Pedro considered and then answered, "I am tired of people always driving me off when they are tired of my tricks. If I'm somewhere I want to be, I want to be able to stay right where I am."

Jesus agreed, but Pedro insisted, "If I want to stay, not even the King of Heaven can make me leave."

A little annoyed (and ready to be done with Pedro Ordimalas), Jesus agreed to this as well and continued on his way with St. Peter.

Pedro took his magical cards and set off on a gambling spree the likes of which no one in Taos had ever seen. His wife and children starved to death waiting for him to bring his winnings home. Jesus saw this and got mad. He sent Death Who Rides a White Horse off on his bony steed to collect Pedro.

When Pedro saw the dark figure on the skeleton horse riding up, he went out to meet Death. "I realize my time has come, but I want to make sure the poor come collect my wealth. Please beat this drum to call them here." The Pale Rider thought it a reasonable request and began pounding on the magic drum. No sooner had Death started playing than he realized he could not stop. Before long, he had bargained away another twenty years to the crafty Pedro.

Twenty years of gambling and carousing later, Death with a Scythe came to harvest the sinful soul of Pedro Ordimalas. Pedro won himself another twenty years with the same trick. Twenty years later, Doña Sebastiana, Death Who Rides in a Cart, showed up and shot Pedro before he could get a word out.

Doña Sebastiana, Death Who Comes in a Cart. Santo by Dixon *santero* Horacio Valdez. *Collection of the Smithsonian American Art Museum, gift of Chuck and Jan Rosenak and purchased through the Luisita L. and Franz H. Denghausen Endowment.*

Dead, Pedro found himself in Limbo, where he was assigned to take care of the unbaptized babies. Baptizing babies all day long was terribly dull, so he amused himself by holding the babies under water for long periods of time. The babies had already died, so it didn't hurt them, but they hated Pedro for it. Before long, a delegation of babies went to Heaven to complain.

Jesus was furious when He found out who was causing the trouble and appeared in person before Pedro. "You are so annoying that not even babies like you! Aren't you ashamed? You must go to Purgatory and do penance," he decided.

In Purgatory, sinners prayed and whipped themselves with cholla cactus to expiate their sins. Pedro Ordimalas grabbed a huge branch and started laying about with it, cruelly flagellating the penitents. When they complained, he kindly explained that he was just trying to be helpful and send them to Heaven faster.

Again, Jesus had to intervene, so angry this time that He sent Pedro to Hell. The devils in Hell thought they would keep Pedro busy chopping firewood, but when let loose in the woodpile, he made himself a sticky fistful of piñon sap. He smeared the sap all over the devils' chairs so when they sat down for dinner they would be stuck fast. The devils were furious and summoned Pedro, who sang hymns to them until they sobbed and implored Jesus to rescue them.

"You're trouble wherever you go, Pedro!" complained Jesus. "You will have to tend sheep outside the gates of Heaven. That way no one but the sheep will have to put up with your company, and St. Peter can keep an eye on you." So Pedro was exiled and became very meek and obedient for a while.

One day, Pedro approached St. Peter and begged for a peek at Heaven, pleading, "Have mercy on me, St. Peter. I will be satisfied for all eternity if you just let me have one look."

St. Peter, who had been favorably impressed with Pedro's care of the sheep, finally gave in. But as soon as he opened the gates, Pedro slipped inside.

St. Peter tried to drag him back out, and Jesus Himself came to force the troublemaker to leave, but Pedro reminded them of their promise that "not even the King of Heaven" could make Pedro leave a place where he wanted to stay. Resigned, Jesus turned Pedro Ordimalas into a rock, so even if he couldn't be driven out of Heaven, at least he wouldn't be up to mischief. As the story goes, Pedro the rock was very happy in Heaven, listening to the angels sing.

PEDRO THE COYOTE

One traditional Taos tale blends Coyote and Pedro Ordimalas into a single trickster. Pedro the Coyote Man was traveling as usual, headed down the road looking for trouble. He met a burro walking slowly, burdened by a large cheese strapped on his back. Pedro wanted that cheese very badly and thought he had better pretend to be lame and ask for a ride. The burro refused Pedro, fearing that the coyote would eat the cheese.

"Oh, no, no, my friend, I would never do that. I am a good man, ask anybody! You know, I don't even like cheese." Coyote insisted and argued, and finally the burro gave in and let him climb up. Pedro Coyote chattered about trivial matters as he rode in order to distract from the fact that he was gradually loosening the strings that held the cheese on the burro's back. When he had it loose, he threw the cheese onto the roadside.

Finally, they arrived at the coyote's house, and as Pedro dismounted, the burro realized the cheese was gone. Knowing he would be blamed, the burro

Donkeys, mules and horses were common trade goods in Taos. Jane Abrams print of Ila McAfee's *We're On the Jury*. *CSWR*.

angrily accused Pedro of stealing the cheese. Coyote rejected the accusation and offered evidence of his innocence. "No, look at my teeth, how clean they are. I told you, I am a good man. I never eat cheese." When the poor burro finally left, Pedro quickly ran back and retrieved the cheese from the road where he had thrown it. He was very happy!

When the burro returned to the farm, the farmer was livid and beat the burro with a stick. "I warned you to look out for Pedro, but you did not listen!" he shouted. When the farmer calmed down, he thought of a way to get back at the trickster.

The farmer sent his burro to go lie in the road. Pedro's wife mistook the burro for a hairy buffalo and developed a strong craving for its liver. Overwhelmed with longing for the tender treat, she hustled her coyote husband out of bed and drove him out half naked. As he ran from the house, scrambling to put his clothes on, his wife shouted at him to hurry and get the best meat before anyone else showed up. So Pedro ran down the hill and stuck his hand deep into the animal's anus to grab the liver. The burro squeezed the intruding hand tight and galloped back to the farm. Coyote tried to wiggle his hand free and escape, but it was firmly trapped in the burro's nethers.

The farmer skinned the coyote and sent him home without a coat. By the time Pedro arrived home, he was shivering from the cold and ordered his wife to build a roaring fire. But when he lay by the fire, his flesh began to roast, and his children couldn't resist the delicious smell. They ate him up, every last bite!

THE LAST WITCHES

Witch problems persisted in New Mexican pueblos and villages long after the Americans came. To their horror, New Mexicans came to discover that they could no longer prosecute witches under the new judicial system.

In 1853, four men from Nambé were hauled into Santa Fe on charges of murdering two others, who were believed to be witches. The accused, who included the governor of the pueblo and the fiscal, or constable, asserted that the alleged witches had been eating babies. They further claimed that they had seen the witches draw infant bones out of their mouths and noses. The baffled judge dismissed the charges for lack of jurisdiction.

Woman in fringed shawl. Jane Abrams print. *CSWR*.

About the same time, a man was arrested in Taos on charges of witchcraft. Officials bound the prisoner over to the United States District Court so that justice could be served, American style. They were soon to be disappointed. The district attorney explained to the frustrated prosecutor that witchcraft was not a crime under American law. When the people of Taos realized that their new government would not protect them from sorcery, they ultimately took matters into their own hands and simply lynched suspected witches.

II

COLONY IN CONFLICT

Off to a Bad Start

As soon as the Spanish colonists in Mexico heard of the rich lands and civilized tribes of New Mexico, a number of explorers launched expeditions—both sanctioned and unsanctioned—into the northern lands. Not all the Spanish explorers made it as far north as Taos. Some were drawn instead to the attractions of the rich and populous middle Rio Grande and Galisteo Basin regions, and some were daunted by the cold weather, mountainous terrain and threat of "wild tribes."

In 1591, Don Gaspar Castaño de Sosa, the governor of Nuevo Léon, led one unauthorized expedition that included two hundred men, as well as women and children, in search of rich mines. Despite traveling in mid-January, the men of the expedition made it all the way to Taos Pueblo. Far from welcoming the strangers, the Taos people were "distinctly hostile," refusing admittance to the Spanish men. They indicated that the visitors were to sleep far from the pueblo, in an area reserved for traders from the Plains.

In the morning, Sosa again tried to gain admittance to the pueblo and considered attacking to "reduce it to obedience." Although Sosa's men hauled two small cannons, some members of the group dissuaded Sosa from this rash course of action, and the party retreated to friendlier pueblos in the south. As he left, Castaño de Sosa vowed to come back in the spring when the "reduction" would be easier. Before he could make good on his threat, a

Nicholas Sanson, *Amerique Septentrionale, La Nouveau Mexique et La Florida*, 1650. *Courtesy Library of Congress Geography and Map Division.*

party from Mexico intercepted the colonists and took Sosa into custody for illegal exploration and colonization.

Seven years later, another group of Spanish showed up at Taos. Don Juan de Oñate stopped in briefly to take a vow of obedience and vassalage but then left again, and at first no colonists were attracted to the high, mountainous plateau. Although the Spanish colony did not affect the Taos Pueblo in some ways, its inhabitants still resented the intruders. On another visit from the Spanish, Oñate further infuriated the Taos people when he killed a promising young leader by hurling the youth from the three-story roof of the pueblo. On the defense, the Taos people, with Picurís Pueblo and the Jicarilla Apache, drew closer in opposition to the Spanish. Although the Spanish first noted this alliance in 1609, they did not follow up due to more pressing concerns. Over the next century, the Spanish colonists would learn the hard way what a dangerous force these allies could be.

Troublesome Taxes

The colonists demanded much of New Mexico's indigenous inhabitants. The Spanish system allowed the government to issue a kind of revenue license to landowners who assisted in protecting the colony. In return, the landowners could demand a certain amount of tribute from the pueblos under mission control. This fragile system broke down in hard years, when either adverse weather or raiding tribes decimated the food or cotton supply. Many pueblos still remembered how the demanding Spanish explorers were quick to torch pueblos and slaughter their inhabitants when refused food or cloth. Most pueblos grudgingly complied with the Spanish demands, but in May 1613, the people of Taos surprisingly refused.

At the time, the clergy and the secular government were fiercely battling over the governance of the colony, and the priests were quick to seize the opportunity to criticize the governor, Don Pedro de Peralta, for allowing this to happen. Peralta sent spies to Taos to assess the situation, and they reported that it was a simple misunderstanding because the people who would have made the payments were out on other business when the soldiers came. Peralta assured the priests and the public that nothing was wrong and sent another detachment of soldiers to collect their tithe of woven goods.

Whether the soldiers ultimately managed to collect is unknown but unlikely. As the soldiers traveled past the pueblo of Nambé, the resident mission priest stopped them and made them turn around and return to Santa Fe lest they miss the Pentecost mass. The frustrated governor turned them back north, ordering them to attend mass at one of the northern pueblos. Furious at the governor for presuming to countermand orders from a priest, the (self-appointed and shady) head of the church in New Mexico excommunicated the governor, causing a catastrophic rift between the colonists and missionaries.

Most *encomiendas*, as these kinds of fiefdoms were known, were profitable and fairly coveted. But Taos and Hopi earned reputations as "punishment" posts, for the holder of the encomienda had to patrol a wild, uncivilized frontier among the most resentful and menacing of the pueblos. Not a few Spaniards and some priests complained about being "banished" to Taos for crossing the governor. One governor even used an undesirable encomienda to rid himself of an inconvenient husband while he wooed the wife in Santa Fe. Others who "won" the Taos encomienda included both the insubordinate and the notorious.

MISERABLE MISSIONARIES

The people of the Taos Pueblo enjoyed a few years of peace before the first mission priest arrived. Fray Francisco de Zamora was the first priest to be assigned, but it was probably Fray Pedro de Miranda who oversaw the construction of the mission of San Geronimo. Miranda came to Taos in 1617 and served there on and off for the rest of his life, keeping his flock in superstitious thrall. Along with Father Miranda came a few families of Spanish settlers, who lived in the pueblo at first and eventually moved just south of the pueblo's lands.

One story of the early days of Spanish settlement in Taos is that the people of the pueblo were at first very welcoming to the colonists and offered them rooms in the pueblo. This warm welcome lasted until the first interracial couple started courting. Alarm on both sides prompted the settlers to remove themselves to Ranchos de Taos, a suitably chaste distance from the natives. Although settlers eventually built a chapel in their settlement (which the mission priests periodically visited), they continued to attend mass in San Geronimo. Despite the best efforts of priests, parents and elders, young people from both cultures continued to flirt when they got the chance.

Santo of Santiago. Jane Abrams print from a carving made by Carlos Vierra for *El Crepúsculo*, July 1950. *CSWR.*

Miranda's first decade was difficult, but a stroke of luck enabled him to preserve his position. He had imposed strict sexual norms on the women of the pueblo. Some women were content to conform to his requirement of monogamy, and even to marry in the church, but others didn't think Miranda had *any* business in *their* business. While debating this point among friends, one advocate of resisting the sexual restrictions was struck by lightning (described by the Franciscans as coming out of a "clear and serene" sky). This incident convinced the Taos people to give the priest a second chance, and "all who were secretly in concubinage got married and believed sincerely all that the Father taught them."

When an inspector from the church came to look over the mission, he found a somewhat rebellious populace that nonetheless boasted a suspiciously high number of converts and two priests cheerfully engaged in a rapid expansion of the church holdings. This happy situation did not last long, as the industrious Italian priest left for warmer climes and Miranda went to serve elsewhere in New Mexico. Fray Nicolás Hidalgo took over as the mission priest.

Fray Miranda inspired a rash of weddings and some faithful converts, but Fray Nicolás Hidalgo, who also served in the 1630s, brought pain and misery to his flock. From the records that remain, we know that Hidalgo was a cruel sexual predator, tormenting fathers and sons, as well as the women of the pueblo. One petitioner to the governor claimed that Hidalgo was practicing both castration and sodomy among the Pueblo men. Pedro Acomilla claimed that Hidalgo had beaten him and then twisted his penis so cruelly that it "broke in half." Twisting and squeezing a father's testicles was part of Hidalgo's technique for demonstrating the man's impotence in front of his sons in order to undermine their sense of filial obligation. He insisted that he used this approach to punish the haughty Taos men and make them meek, humble and gentle.

The following year, a young woman named Isabel Yantula produced a four-year-old fathered by Hidalgo. She told a sorry story of how Hidalgo had murdered her husband so he could rape her. Another woman, Margita Tultamy, brought forth a one-year-old also fathered by Fray Hidalgo and kept hidden in the convent. Perhaps these sexual transgressions were less easily overlooked, for Fray Miranda was sent back to Taos to replace the hated Hidalgo.

Miranda returned to find that Hidalgo's brutality had wiped out the pueblo's respect for the priesthood. The people were angry, giving voice to one story after another about their mistreatment and humiliation at Hidalgo's hands. Unwisely, Miranda took his fellow priest's side and chastised his congregation for speaking ill of a priest. This hardened the people against the missionary, whom they had formerly respected.

Shortly after Christmas 1639, some men of the pueblo killed Father Miranda and the two soldiers who guarded him and befouled and profaned

Pueblo-style church. Jane Abrams print. *CSWR.*

the Eucharist. Not satisfied, they also demolished both the church and the convent. Fully fired up, they rode on to Picurís Pueblo to kill the friar there, but he was fortunate enough to be elsewhere. Perhaps the long ride to Picurís sobered their bloodlust, or perhaps they feared the Spanish response, but the men involved did not continue their rampage. Like many Taos, Picurís and Jicarillas who angered the Spanish, they fled to Cuartelejo, an outpost on the Arkansas River in what is now southwest Kansas. Cuartelejo was too far for Spanish pursuit, and if not actually within the boundary of New France, it was a lawless borderland of French traders and various Plains tribes.

Lacking criminals to punish and hang, the ecclesiastic leadership was quick to lay blame for Miranda's assassination at the feet of the governor. The people of Jemez had similarly murdered their priest, and the father custodian, head of the church in New Mexico, did not believe this was coincidence. The fathers claimed that the governor, Luís de Rosas, had commanded the Indians not to obey the priests. The furor the clergy whipped up against Rosas eventually resulted in his assassination.

If they had been less determined to press their political advantage, the priests might have considered that Taos and Jemez were unhappy for other reasons. Rosa's activities as a slaver disrupted trade with friendly Apaches, Utes and Navajos, provoking them into raiding the missions. The Spanish had brought smallpox with them, which had recently devastated the populace, and the Spanish prayers did not prevent widespread death and suffering. Physical and sexual abuse on top of death and disease was just too much. During this period, seven or eight Indians were hanged on suspicion of insurrection, after which the Spanish mistakenly thought that the "restlessness ceased."

Reforms and Repression

Restlessness had not ceased. The men of Taos Pueblo had developed a plan for a general, colony-wide revolt by 1650. As an aid for enlisting support from the other pueblos, the plotters sewed two finely cured and softened deerskins together, painting the plan on the hides. Traveling through the pueblos with this guide, messengers enlisted support from everyone but the Hopi. Other pueblos considered the Hopi critical to an uprising, so the people of Taos simmered down and continued to suffer the presence of Spanish in their pueblo and their valley.

Getting rid of Hidalgo and Miranda hadn't improved the plight of the people of Taos. The new missionaries forced the people of the pueblo to start building another church for the mission of San Geronimo. Men particularly resented being made to do the traditionally women's work of plastering, insisting that such work was emasculating.

One of the friars assigned to Taos died suddenly in 1658. The Inquisition launched a swift investigation and then just as quickly backpedaled when stories of the friar's appalling behavior came to light. The case was dropped, and the suspected murderer, named Francisco, was released. Later, information revealed that Francisco had been party to Miranda's assassination. Far from hiding this fact, he danced at a ceremonial while wearing Miranda's vestments.

Many of the men who had fled Taos after killing Fray Miranda returned during the stormy, two-year administration of Governor Bernardo López de Mendizábal. López earned the undying enmity of the priests by giving more liberties to the Pueblo people of New Mexico. His reforms included establishing a minimum wage for Indian labor and permitting *kachina* dances again. In part to trade and in part to strengthen the northern frontier, he sent an expedition to bring the refugees back to Taos. He eventually appointed Francisco, Miranda's murderer, as governor of the pueblo, further enraging the clergy.

Did López's reforms or the killing of Fray Miranda reduce the brutal conditions for the Taos Pueblo? They didn't help the woman who was raped and beaten to death by a different friar the following year. Apparently, she had not done satisfactory work while spinning cotton for the priest, sending him into a murderous rage. Both the governor and his wife investigated the case. They were so appalled that Governor López reported the abuse immediately to the vice custodian, who imprisoned the priest for several months before exiling him from the colony.

Taos dancers. Jane Abrams print from a carving made by D.H. Lawrence for *Laughing Horse* 13 (1926). *CSWR.*

In part for their trouble in removing this monster from New Mexico, both López and his wife were arrested and imprisoned by the Inquisition for violating ecclesiastical immunity—that is, for presuming to have judicial oversight over the clergy. Although López protested that he had merely passed the case against the friar along to the vice custodian, the inquisitors pointed out he had no right even to investigate the charges. Governor López died in prison while awaiting trial for this and many similar "crimes" against the church.

During the subsequent two decades, the religious and secular authorities continued to clash. When priests gained ascendancy, they conducted brutal purges in the pueblos, confiscating and burning sacred masks, fetishes and other items. When the governors gained ascendancy, they engaged in equally brutal approaches to making money: slave trading and forced labor among the pueblos.

One governor, perhaps trying to pacify the Franciscans, arrested several men on charges of witchcraft. Warriors descended on Santa Fe and barged right into the governor's chambers in a successful bid to intimidate him into releasing the prisoners. One of the men released was a Tewa from San Juan Pueblo named Popé.

Popé Makes a Plan

Upon his release, Popé did not return to San Juan but sought refuge in Taos, where he could plan in secret. During this time, he lived with a Taos man named Jhaka. While praying in a kiva, Popé saw a vision of three fiery beings, who told him how to coordinate a revolt that would drive the hated Spanish from the land. Each pueblo in the kingdom was to receive a *palmilla* cord tied with a certain number of knots. Every day, the warriors of that pueblo should untie one knot, and when the last knot was untied, it would be time to rise up together and kill their oppressors.

The cords were prepared, and the Taos people sent their fastest runners south. They carried a message: anyone who did not agree with the pact would be destroyed for treason. Pueblos that planned to participate were instructed to signal their acquiescence with smoke. One by one, the pueblos agreed to Popé's plan.

On August 10, 1680, the people of Taos began their slaughter by killing Fray Antonio de Mora and Fray Juan de Pedrosa, the two priests assigned to the Mission of San Geronimo de Taos. At the same time, the Picurís killed their priests. Both pueblos burned the missions and desecrated any sacramental objects they could find. Warriors spread out and began a systematic slaughter of the seventy-five or so Spanish settlers in the area.

The rebels burned fields and plundered the homesteads. The ransacked houses were put to the torch, and the angry men shot or hacked down every man, woman and child they encountered. Their bloody work done, the warriors rode in a body down to Santa Fe to root out the Spanish from the capital. The Taos and Picurís were welcome reinforcements for the sieging forces, and with their help, the rebels were able to take a hill behind the Palace of the Governors, from which they could shoot at the terrified Spanish cowering in the fortified building.

Encouraged by the arrival of the northern tribes, the siege of Santa Fe continued. The attackers roamed around the villa seeking to obliterate

Indian warrior. Jane Abrams print from a carving made by Pedro Barela for *Laughing Horse* 15 (1928).

all traces of the enemy. They sacked the church and burned the remains, defiled the cemetery and obliterated a number of houses. Warriors and other Indians from all over the province kept streaming into the capital to join in the purge. Eventually, the Spanish colonists made a break for it, and the native people allowed them to leave, fervently hoping they would never return.

Only a handful of people, out of scores of colonists, escaped the carnage of Taos. Diego Lucero de Godoy was in El Paso when thirty-two members of his family and household staff were slaughtered. He never returned to New Mexico. The others were the *sargento mayor*, Fernando Duran y Chaves, and his teenaged son, Cristobal. Chaves and Cristobal had taken an Andalusian guest of theirs out for the day, leaving Señora Chaves at home with her younger children and the visiting family. When the men returned, not a living soul remained. In a panic, they left their wives and children lying dead where they fell and snuck out of the district past the fearsome, enraged warriors. For seven days, the trio fled through the mountains. Finally, they reached the besieged Villa of Santa Fe, under heavy fire from the Taos, Picurís and other nations. Unable to find refuge in Santa Fe, they continued south and met some other refugees at Isleta three days later. None of the settlers from the Picurís region survived. The Chaves party brought the first news of conditions in Santa Fe and elsewhere to the settlers fleeing the middle and lower Rio Grande Valleys, the Salinas District and the Galisteo Basin.

Cristobal soon joined the army and left for patrol in Sonora. Chaves never returned to New Mexico and never learned that he had left behind two daughters living in the carnage. Apparently, Chaves had a more complex marital life than your average Joe. We do not know the name of the wife who was killed, but we do know the name of his "other" wife: Elena Ruiz Caceres. Don Fernando conceived at least two children with her: Maria and Josefa. Whether they were captured or rescued, the girls had moved into the pueblo and become young women by the time the Spanish returned to Taos. One daughter married a prominent member of the Martín family. At the prenuptial investigation, she swore that her birth was legitimate. Whether or not this was true, there was absolutely no one left to contradict her.

The alliance among the pueblos did not last long, and in the absence of the Spanish, the Plains tribes stepped up their raids. Popé might have returned to Taos, but infighting sapped his power. Nevertheless, the Taos people may have been delighted to hear that some Spaniards came and quickly left again. They were certainly dismayed to hear several years later that the Spanish were back—possibly for good.

Reconquest and Revolt

The new governor, Don Diego de Vargas, had won peace with many other pueblos before he came to Taos in 1692. The Taos governor—deeply unhappy to see the hated regime returned—nevertheless swore allegiance to the Spanish king at Vargas' command. The church dispatched a new missionary, who initiated the construction of a new church. The natives started to feel like all the errors of the past were being repeated. Within two years, Taos Pueblo was in open revolt again.

De Vargas found the pueblo deserted upon his return to Taos in 1694. Fearing retribution, the residents had fled to a nearby canyon. They refused to negotiate with the Spanish and maintained a stubborn silence for a full year, until the governor finally persuaded all the Taos people to return to their pueblo.

The following year, rebellion broke out again, and the Taos mission became the scene of a bloody martyrdom. The martyr was Fray Antonio Carboneli, one of five priests killed during the 1696 revolt. The other priest at Taos, along with the soldiers guarding the mission, fled through the dark night to Picurís. This time, the people of Picurís were spared in the uprising. Elsewhere, priests were burned alive in their churches, and twenty-one colonists were slain. Once again, Governor de Vargas rode to Taos, but the

Skeleton and tree riddled with arrows. *From George D. Brewerton, "Ride with Kit Carson,"* Harper's New Monthly Magazine *(August 1853).*

time for negotiating was over. He led a party that included one hundred Pecos warriors and relentlessly pursued the rebels. The Taos people had once again fled into a canyon, and there, Vargas fought them. In October, the warriors of Taos Pueblo finally surrendered and returned to their home, vowing to keep the peace with the Spaniards.

Only one person in Taos ended up getting punished for his role in the revolt. When Governor Otermín tried to reclaim the province two years after his unceremonious flight from Santa Fe, he captured and interrogated several people. The Spanish were baffled and frustrated in determining the reasons behind the revolt. As good Catholics, they couldn't understand why the "pacified" Indians had turned against the true faith. Perhaps Otermín sought a cause other than his own failure in leadership.

Otermín questioned Juan Cucala from Taos about why he "returned to the ancient idolatry of his ancestors" and committed "murders, rapes and other atrocities." The man replied that he did not have a good heart. Otermín pressed him to justify the "treacherous murders, atrocious robbery of churches and burnings of sacred things and images," but Cucala refused to give his interrogator any satisfaction, persistently repeating that everything he had done "was because of a bad heart." Although some of the rebels received death sentences, Cucala's sentence was four years of slavery.

III

RAIDERS AND TRADERS

The northern border of New Mexico abutted the southwestern border of French-held Louisiana until the Americans bought the land in 1804. No one was quite sure where Louisiana stopped and New Mexico started. A common demarcation—which persisted through American acquisition of the land—was the Rio Napeste, or today's Arkansas River. Spanish cartographers placed the Louisiana border at the Mississippi, but French cartographers drew it just north of Taos.

It's hard to say how much Old World rivalries fed into New World animosity. However, starting in the 1700s, the French traders near New Mexico began a policy of arming select tribes. The Spanish were firm about prohibiting firearms for native people, so when the French sold guns to the Pawnee and Comanche, New Mexicans found themselves at a terrible disadvantage. Not only were most of the people on the border without guns, but also the Spanish harquebuses were antiquated, clumsy and slow to load.

When the "Buffalo Eaters" started attacking northern New Mexico settlements with firearms, the shock galvanized the governor. By 1710, Governor José Chacon Villaseñor granted the first families land south of Taos Pueblo and along the Rio de las Trampas. Times were desperate, and New Mexican officials could no longer adhere to the laws specifying that only families of pure Spanish blood could receive boons of this nature (land grants were made in the king's name, so the recipients had to be worthy). The Romero family, who settled south of Taos Pueblo in today's

The churchyard of the Penitente morada, Taos NM. John Collier, photographer. *Library of Congress, Prints & Photographs Division, FSA-OWI Collection, LC-USW3-013803-C DLC.*

Ranchos de Taos, were self-described *coyotes*, or three-quarters native and one-quarter Spanish.

The Spanish caste system, along with census reports and marriage investigations, gives us a fair idea of who was settling on the northern border in those days. Plenty of *mestizos* (Indian mother and Spanish father) and *coyotes* settled at the fringes of New Mexico, but the caste that predominated in New Mexico border towns was unknown elsewhere in New Spain. The caste term *genízaro* usually describes a descendant of a nomadic tribe who had been acculturated into Spanish customs.

The Spanish had hoped to acculturate the surrounding "savage nations" with the force of their faith and technology or, failing that, with generous gifts. This strategy was never entirely successful, requiring the Spanish colonists to adopt a new strategy that involved "ransoming" children from these tribes and raising them to be Christians. Slavery in New Mexico had always been illegal, but many families acquired

A *coyote* is the child of a *mestizo* man and an Indian woman. Painting by Manuel Cabrera, 1763. *From the Antiguo Colegio de San Ildefonso in Mexico City.*

criados, or servants, in this manner, which essentially amounted to slave trafficking.

The supply of captives to be "ransomed" was critical. Both Spanish frontiersmen and warlike Plains tribes did a brisk business raiding Apache,

A painting depicting all the possible caste combinations in New Spain. Marriage investigations took the racial and caste heritage of each member of the couple into account. *Courtesy of the Museo Nacional del Virreinato, Tepotzotlán, Mexico.*

Ute and Navajo encampments for children. Because these tribes still bitterly remembered the aggressive slave trading of seventeenth-century governors, this new practice seemed like confirmation that the Spanish people would never treat native people fairly. The acquisition and treatment of the genízaros remained a sore point for the Navajo, Ute, Plains tribes and Apache through the nineteenth century.

One early nineteenth-century New Mexican painted a picture of how this slavery worked in practice, probably unchanged from the methods of eighteenth-century slavers:

Pawnee and French soldiers coming out of the woods to attack the Spanish. From a painting made on bison hide depicting the August 1720 skirmish. *Image of Segesser hide courtesy of New Mexico History Museum and Palace of the Governors.*

> *On arriving home after a slaving expedition, the first thing to do was to take the children to the priest to baptize them and give them a name. They would naturally take your name and as they grew up they would consider you and your wife as their parents. If you did not have the pluck to go after Indian children yourself you could buy one for five hundred dollars. It must be remembered that many parties that went after servants never returned. The Indians killed them all.*

Within a decade after the original land grants were issued, more settlers started pouring into the Taos Valley. One prominent family, the Martíns, relocated from Abiquiu in 1716 and were granted a generous parcel that, until the Pueblo Revolt, belonged to Diego Lucero de Godoy. The new settlers' mettle was soon put to the test, as Comanches raided Don Fernando de Taos, skillfully riding their Spanish horses and wielding their French weapons.

Upon hearing the news, the governor sent Pedro de Villasur with over one hundred troops to scout out the French position. Leaving Taos, Villasur led his men deep into the Plains. They rode as far as the Platte River in present-day Nebraska before encountering a Pawnee encampment that might have been hosting French traders. Villasur halted nearby, but his hesitation was fatal. The Pawnee swept down on the Spaniards at daybreak and caught them unmounted, unarmed and entirely unprepared for the massacre. By lunchtime, Villasur lay dead, as did the party's interpreter and chief of scouts.

The bedraggled party that finally returned to New Mexico was proof that an offensive policy was doomed to failure, so the viceroy fixed on a defensive policy: building a *presidio* at the outpost of Cuartelejo. The Cuartelejo fort would have patrolled and enforced the border along the Rio Napeste, but the idea withered on the vine. For the next century, the idea of building a presidio at or near Taos was proposed by one governor after another, only to be rejected by one Mexican bureaucrat after another.

THE WAR ON SMUGGLING

By 1723, a new plan had been put into effect, which was to outlaw any trade whatsoever with the French. As part of the same strategy, the governor allowed trade with the Plains tribes only at the settlements of Taos or Pecos. The resulting Taos trade fair became an institution, frequented by Comanche, Kiowa, Ute and Apache traders. The Taos Valley proved to be ideal for growing wheat, and the settlers exchanged their surplus

wheat, produce and wool for horses, buffalo products and "ransomed" captives. Sometimes they were reduced to buying back their own children and horses; at other times, they were happy to buy captives and animals stolen from others.

This profitable trade in people—not to mention stolen livestock—escalated frontier hostilities. At the time, the Comanche were trying to expand their territory and viciously attacked the encampment of the Jicarilla Apache in an effort to control hunting on the Plains northeast of Taos. The Comanche carried off half the Jicarilla women and children and killed all but sixty-nine men and three boys. It is possible, but unlikely, that some of the captured children were sold into Taos households. The governor suggested that the decimated Jicarilla could move into Don Fernando de Taos, but none of the parties concerned was thrilled with this idea.

Instead, a new mission was established on the Rio de las Trampas. In exchange for protection, the Jicarilla were expected to stop their buffalo hunting. This crushed the fledgling settlement economically, and when the hungry Apaches heard that the entire Spanish garrison was mobilizing, they fled in panic. Some moved down to Pecos, where they could still access the buffalo plains. Others moved into the mountains and eventually joined bands of Utes and even the enemy Comanche.

For some time, the Spanish government attempted to round up the Jicarilla and move them back to Taos, but the effort "was frustrated unhappily, because fear swayed them." At this point, the Apaches feared the Spanish as

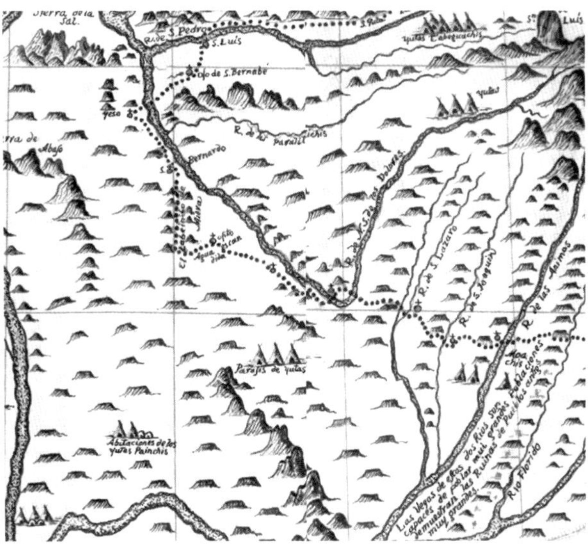

On the Dominguez-Escalante expedition, Miera y Pacheco noted a number of Ute camps in the Four Corners area. Taos raiders frequently ventured into this lawless zone for captives. *Plano geografico, de la tierra descubierta, y demarcada por Don Bernardo de Miera, y Pacheco. 1776.*

much as anyone, thanks to the unstoppable slave trade. By 1748, the Jicarilla had migrated west, leaving Taos without a buffer against northern raiders.

The Taos community could ill afford to lose the Jicarilla, and other communities were similarly caught up in the strife caused by human trafficking. In 1741, the Governor Don Gaspar Domingo de Mendoza specifically addressed the trade in women and children with a *bando* (proclamation) prohibiting attacks on defenseless women and children (and gambling, as an afterthought). The governor expected the Spanish colonists to behave as Catholic gentlemen and imposed a stiff, three-hundred-silver-peso fine on any men caught mistreating, wounding or killing "infidel" women, boys or girls, followed by six years in exile. The governor's bando was well intentioned but impossible to enforce, particularly in distant Taos.

Before long, it became clear that no one was the least bit interested in enforcing this law. The baptisms of captured children continued, with the Navajo, Ute, Comanche and Apache tribes bearing the greatest losses of youth. Just three years after the bando was passed, a relative of the Taos Martíns baptized nine stolen Indian children. Far from being an outlaw, Captain Sebastian Martín was considered to be a true *caballero* and a pillar of society.

French Menace the Borders

A group of Comanche men paid Taos Pueblo a friendly visit in 1748, catalyzing a wave of panic about the French that reached the viceroy in Mexico City. The New Mexicans weren't worried about the Comanche as much as they were concerned about the French arming the Comanche.

One winter day, seven Comanche came to Taos Pueblo to trade for tobacco and to notify everyone concerned that their band would be planning to visit the valley "as soon as the snow shall decrease in the mountains." Meanwhile, the Comanche, at their *ranchería*, were tanning buffalo hides and entertaining thirty-three Frenchmen. They also happened to mention that the French had armed them with "plenty of muskets." Anticipating that the Spanish might launch an expedition to pursue the French, the Comanche added that the majority of French traders had already left for parts unknown, but two traders would be coming into New Mexico in the spring.

When the news reached Governor Mendoza, he shot a letter off to his superiors in Mexico City. In it, he wrote that if the French were able

to "insinuate themselves into this kingdom," they would "cause some uprising." To jog the viceroy's memories, Mendoza revisited a traumatic episode from six years earlier, when a Frenchman named Luís María and his eight companions arrived at Taos via the "same route as the Jicarilla." The governor recounted complacently that after the hapless Frenchman was "shot in the public square…of Santa Fe," the remaining French intruders fled New Mexico for the hospitably trackless anonymity of the Plains. The French traders had been accused of starting an uprising, possibly by violating the ban on trading firearms to the indigenous New Mexicans.

He finished by proposing—neither for the first nor the last time—a northern presidio to protect the population of Taos. Rather than siting it all the way out at Cuartelejo, he suggested a closer location: the site of the abandoned Jicarilla Apache settlement. The presidio could use the many shelters built by the departed Jicarilla. In case the viceroy didn't know why the Apache homes were abandoned, the governor reminded him that it was the Comanche—now equipped with new, high-tech muskets instead of antiquated harquebuses—who had decimated the Jicarilla population, "despoiling them, killing most of them."

The Mexican authorities might have felt that worrying about thirty men who possibly visited a distant camp some time ago was tantamount to hysterical paranoia, for no action was taken to protect the northern frontier and Taos, then or ever. But the governor's fears were well justified. With French firearms, either the Comanche or the Pueblo might drive the Spanish from the province again.

Strangely, when the two French traders reached Santa Fe, Governor Mendoza not only offered them a lavish reception but also allowed them to leave unmolested—and more importantly—with cartographic information about the Spanish settlements. The traders brought this information back to Louisiana, which did not sit well with the Spanish government. Soon, Mendoza's era of peacemaking came to an end.

Thanks to trade fairs (and flouting official policy), the Spanish colonists finally acquired French guns of their own. As the technology improved, the warfare escalated. The fact of the matter was that the Comanche skill with horses and guns outstripped everyone else. The cartographer Miera y Pacheco wrote, "They [the Comanche] acquired horses and weapons of iron, and they have had so much practice in the management of horses and arms, that they excel all other tribes in agility and spirit, making themselves lords and masters of all the buffalo country, wresting it from the Apache Nation."

A Comanche horse game. Horsemanship was one of the ways the Comanche gained supremacy on the southern Plains. *George Catlin,* Notes and Travels Amongst the North American Indians, *1913.*

As the trade in stolen horses diminished with the Plains tribes, men from northern New Mexico began trading stolen horses along the Old Spanish Trail. Jane Abrams print. *CSWR.*

A few years later, a new governor cracked down on trade outside the province. Between the slave raids and the firearms, there was too much danger. Celebrants at the Taos feast days that year were advised by the governor's messenger that commerce with the "Cumanches" carried a fine of five hundred pesos and that it was a hanging offense to go more than a league from the pueblo unless authorized to do so.

What were the Taos traders doing that was so dangerous that it warranted the death penalty? The record doesn't say, but the central Spanish government was notoriously strict when it came to closing the borders, and Mendoza's security lapses had attracted negative attention from the viceroy. Perhaps there was also an element of suppressing rituals and other alliances that Taos shared with the Plains people.

The new bando was as unenforceable as the last, and by 1750, the trade fairs had resumed. After a peaceful fair that year, the Comanche took their new horses and rode them south in a brutal raid against Galisteo Pueblo. The peace was so fragile that it hardly deserved the name. Again, calls were made to fortify the frontier, this time with new settlements, but pleas to the Spanish government were like dropping stones in a well for all the impact they had.

MASSACRE AT VILLALPANDO

For a decade, Taoseños kept an uneasy peace with the Comanche. Trade fairs continued to everyone's benefit—except that of the captives, sold into lives of servitude. Groups of men from the pueblo and the settlements ventured unmolested into the Plains for buffalo hunts. According to legend, relations were so warm that a settler named Pablo de Villalpando promised his daughter in marriage to a Comanche chief but not so warm that Villalpando actually went through with the deal. He permitted his Rosa to marry a Spaniard instead: Juan José Jaquez.

The stories and songs about Maria Rosa de Villalpando paint her as an innocent beauty for whom the Comanche chief longed at any price. Whether wrathful over the breach of promise or the spectacle of Taos warriors dancing with Comanche scalps at the recent trade fair, three thousand Comanche warriors rode down into the valley one quiet August night in 1760. The alarm was sounded throughout the settlements along the Rio Fernando de Taos, and several families gathered at the hacienda of the Villalpando family.

War dance. Jane Abrams print from a carving made by Antonio Archuleta for *Laughing Horse* 16 (Summer 1929). *CSWR*.

Like many haciendas on the frontiers of New Mexico, Pedro de Villalpando had built a *torreón*, or watchtower, in his compound, useful as both a lookout and a defensive structure. The fourteen Spanish men of the party armed themselves and took to the heights with bows and arrows, rocks and whatever else would help them deter the attack.

An engineer who wrote of the rout several years later blamed the structure and siting of the torreón, which not only allowed the Comanche warriors to shield themselves from the Spaniards' volleys but also enabled them to pick off the Spanish archers emerging to loose their arrows. It seems inconceivable that fourteen men could have held their own against the thousands of warriors surging at their walls, no matter how well engineered the building could have been.

Regardless, the Comanche gained access to the torreón and killed every Spanish man without hesitation, including Señor Villalpando and Juan Jaquez. Breaking down the gates of the hacienda, the Comanche found a number of women ready to fight like men. Señora Villalpando defended her home with a lance until she was slain. When there was no one left to fight, the Comanche rounded up the survivors—between fifty and sixty-five women and children—and marched them off for points unknown. The captives included the orphaned and widowed Maria Rosa. Her two-year-old son, José Julian, somehow escaped capture and remained in Taos to be raised by neighbors.

To rescue the unfortunates, the governor quickly sent presidial soldiers, Jicarilla warriors (who were still nursing grudges against the Comanche) and any citizens capable of bearing arms. After searching for about forty days without finding a trace of the raiders, the dispirited and hungry scouts returned.

The next summer, the Comanche returned to Taos with seven captives. They wanted to reopen trade and felt that the hostages were an excellent mark of goodwill. The Spanish thought differently. By order of the governor, the negotiators were taken hostage. One was killed, and several were wounded in the scuffle. Then, contrary to established protocols for negotiations, the Spanish turned their cannons and muskets on the assembled Comanche men, women and children.

This excessive, vicious attack killed four hundred Comanche. Some Ute who were in Taos for trade took advantage of the chaos to steal about one thousand Comanche horses and three Comanche women. Both the injuries and the insults fanned the conflict into a hot war. The governor's superiors decried his use of force because the bad faith the Spanish showed at the trade fair undermined years of delicate peace negotiations.

During this difficult period, the colonists moved into the pueblo for protection. Bishop Tamarón of Durango paid a visit at this time and found 160 members of thirty-six different Spanish families living in the pueblo. This condition persisted on and off for the next three decades, until the settlers rebuilt their ranchos and plazas. They were adopting recommendations for new defensive architecture and were not going to return to their homes and villages until they could feel safe. To assist the existing settlers in the valley, the governor issued new land grants to families willing to help defend the frontier.

Ten years after the tragedy, Maria Rosa Villalpando surfaced in St. Louis, married to a *voyageur*, or French trader. She had borne a son by her

Fighting the Comanche in their ranchería. *From A.H. Guernsey, "Army Life on the Border,"* Harper's New Monthly Magazine *(September 1866).*

Comanche captors, but perhaps her legendary beauty was enough to draw the eye of prosperous merchant (and one of the city's founding fathers) Jean Salé dit Lajoie. José Julian Villalpando never saw his mother again, though he created a large family of his own. He married a local girl at age twenty-six, and together they raised at least nine children.

THE PRICE OF PEACE

Far to the east, the English colonies declared independence in 1776; changes were afoot in New Mexico as well. The energetic and curious priest Fray Atanasio Dominguez followed an exhaustive survey of, and report on, the New Mexico missions with an expedition to explore routes to California. The peaceful expedition fell far short of California, although Dominguez, with fellow priest Silvestre Vélez de Escalante, did open relations with

Don Bernardo Miera y Pacheco showed the Alcaldia de Taos at the northeastern border of New Mexico. *From* Plano de la Provincia Interna de el Nuebo Mexico, *1779. Library of Congress Geography and Map Division.*

tribes as far north as Utah Lake. Thanks to cartographer Bernardo Miera y Pacheco, the Dominguez-Escalante expedition added greatly to the colony's geographical knowledge and ultimately laid the foundation for the Old Spanish Trail, which opened commerce to the Pacific coast.

New Mexican governor Juan Bautista de Anza. *Portrait from Dr. H.E. Bolton,* The Spanish Borderlands, *1921.*

In 1778, the viceroy appointed Juan Bautista de Anza as the new governor. He left his distinguished position in Sonora (which included modern-day Arizona) to govern New Mexico. Anza was a highly capable leader, brilliant explorer and military tactician—just what New Mexicans needed.

Anza began launching attacks against hostile bands of Comanche. For two years, he harassed them with whatever troops and arms he could muster in the impoverished colony. Then, in 1779, Comanche raiders swooped down on Taos, indiscriminately laying waste to Spanish and Pueblo cornfields. Fortunately, the new defensive structures did their job, and the citizens worked together to protect their community. The warriors attacked, were repulsed, retreated to contemplate the situation until the next morning and then departed entirely. Anza reported ten deaths among the natives and one among the Spanish—a young man was killed when he spotted a horse wandering in a cornfield and thought he might be able to capture it.

In retaliation, Anza led a great expedition, including many Ute and Apache warriors, to confront a large force of Comanche led by Chief Cuerno Verde. The Spanish-led forces won the day, leaving Cuerno Verde and many of his warriors dead in the field. Some bands of Comanche started suing for peace, but Anza held out for seven years, until all the Comanche were united in their desire for lasting peace with New Mexicans.

During the years of Anza's offensive, many bands of Comanche came to Taos pleading for peace or shelter. Some brought gifts of buffalo meat, and some returned hostages. The supplicants were allowed to camp near the pueblo temporarily, but all received the same message: they will have peace when all the Comanche agree to it. The last holdout was the war captain Ecueracapa, and the Taoseños urged all visiting bands to find him and talk him into agreeing to peace. The pressure finally paid off, and Ecueracapa, with other Comanche representatives, signed a lasting treaty at a Pecos Pueblo ceremony in 1786.

One of the provisions of Anza's treaty with the Comanche was the guarantee of free trade fairs in Taos. Another provision involved the establishment of a *fondo de aliados* (fund for allies), also called the *fondo de paz y guerra* (fund for peace and war). Although an unofficial system of placating hostile tribes with gifts had been in place for ages, this was a permanent fund that could be drawn on by frontier settlers who found themselves out-of-pocket for keeping the peace.

One Taos man, Pablo Lucero, received reimbursement from the fund after having to slaughter a fat cow to feed a party of Kiowa who stayed at his house for four days. Sometimes the fondo would be used to recompense the Indians when the Spanish raided their settlements, killed their people or abducted their children. Another time, four *vecinos* (citizens) from Taos killed a Jicarilla Apache man, two women and a small boy "without any cause." The fondo de aliados paid the tribe for their loss.

This somewhat happy state of affairs resulted in the Spanish settlers finally moving out of the pueblo and into a town of their own. In 1796, sixty-three families received the grant of Don Fernando de Taos (named for the possibly polygamous Señor Chaves) in a ceremony conducted by the alcalde mayor. This became the community now known simply as Taos. Other plazas granted at that time include Plaza de San Francisco de Paula (now Lower Ranchitos), Plaza de Nuestra Señora de los Dolores (now Cañon), Plaza de San Francisco (now Ranchos de Taos) and Plaza de Santa Gertrudis (now the La Loma neighborhood). Together, the communities contained over seven hundred people. Despite the newly forged peace, the government supplied new grantees with arrows and firearms "on account of the perils of this place."

SLAVES AND *CIBOLEROS*

Peaceful conditions in Taos lasted a mere twenty years. In 1808, Napoleon invaded Spain and installed his brother on the throne. The Bonapartes were concerned with matters in Europe and had little time for New World problems. As Spain's relations with Mexico began to fray, New Mexicans'

Hunting buffalo from horseback. Jane Abrams print from a carving made by Antonio Archuleta for *Laughing Horse* 18 (September 1930). *CSWR.*

relations with neighboring nations also showed sign of the strain. The fondo de aliados ran dry around 1810, so soldiers returned to patrolling the borders around Taos while the governor again strictly regulated trade with the Plains nations. *Ciboleros*, or buffalo hunters, needed to be in possession of permits and adhere to a long list of regulations.

Fortunately for the traders of Taos, years of peace had become a habit that was hard to break. The Plains trade was more robust than it had ever been. Perhaps it is no coincidence that many of the best ciboleros were either freed slaves or descendants of Christianized captives. The *genizaros* must have enjoyed escaping the boundaries of the strict, caste-conscious Spanish society.

Some ciboleros and other laborers in Taos remained slaves. When the Works Progress Administration (WPA) collected stories from Taos residents in the 1930s, it interviewed two men who had lived as slaves to Spanish ranchers. One man from Peñasco didn't know how he came to live at his master's home, but he had been a slave since the age of eight, herding goats and performing other labor. Another, Simeon Tejada, had worked as a cibolero but never saw a penny of payment for long decades of service.

Other ciboleros, like Manuel Le Fevre, were French. The Bonapartes' influence forced New Mexicans to relax their attitudes against these enemies, and a few Frenchmen settled, or regularly traded, in Taos. Like a true cibolero, Le Fevre hunted his buffalo with a lance and gun, traveling to what is now southern Colorado in pursuit of the massive herds.

Americans traveling on the Santa Fe Trail described well-worn bridle paths etched in the prairie soils by the ciboleros, but that way of life was already disappearing. Another French cibolero complained to Lewis Garrard about the effect of hunting with guns on the buffalo herds. As Garrard told it:

> *"Mais sacré," said he complainingly, with a suppressed heave of the breast, "Les Americans, dey go to de Missouri frontier, de buffalo he ron to de montaigne; the trappare wid his dam fusil, he follow to de Bayon Salade, he ron again. Dans les Montaignes Espagnol, bang, bang! toute la journée! toute la journée! go de sacré voleurs. De bison he leave, parce que des fusils scare im vara moche—ici, là, all de sem—sacreé!"—and while telling it, he worked himself in a great heat, as if the prairie and mountain peaks were made exclusively for Frenchmen and ciboleros, through which to chase buffalo in yelling barbarity forever.*

The treaties had not ended the slave trade on New Mexico's northern frontier. A leading citizen, Don Severino Martinez, trafficked in Ute slaves. In 1816, Martinez and some other Taos men were involved in a complex civil and criminal case that illustrates the role of slavery in the local economy. Martinez had given a fine mule to some neighbors of his who were headed up to the San Luis Valley to trade for slaves. Upon their return, Martinez claimed that his partners had traded his mule for a girl, thinking it belonged to someone else. The traders offered to give Martinez a different mule, but he was more interested in trading for the girl and even offered to throw in another few mules to sweeten the deal.

All this was explained in the courts. The case was resolved without too much animosity and without charges being brought against any of the slavers. Today, this casual approach to bartering for children seems only slightly more troubling than the low price of human life. Child slavery was so normal then that even one priest in Taos, Father Gabriel Ussell, had a slave.

The illegal practice continued into the territorial era, when the American judicial system caught up with local customs. One Mexican judge brought charges against 435 slave owners between 1838 and 1839. In the later part of the nineteenth century, several members of the Mares family of Taos were charged with collectively owning 17 slaves. Vicente Mares, who owned 5 slaves himself, had inherited some from his father, putting the lie to the claim that the criados were a kind of servant.

While the Americans were trying to stamp out slavery, the heavy traffic between Missouri and New Mexico was aggravating the Plains tribes. The last great tragedy between the Taos settlers and the Jicarilla Apache came in 1849. A peaceful wagon train from Missouri was traversing the plains east of Taos when a band of Jicarilla swooped down on them. The Jicarilla twice demanded presents from the traders, who twice refused and rudely drove them from camp. When the Apaches came back a third time, it was to kill the men of the party and abduct the three females: Mrs. Ann White, her daughter and her servant.

A group of New Mexicans came across the site of the massacre and also were killed while picking through the wreckage of the wagon train. Only one member of that party survived—a wounded Mexican boy—and he sounded the alarm to the next arriving party. The Americans reported the killings, and the news spread to Taos, along with reports of a $1,000 reward for the return of Ann White.

The First Cavalry, led by Captain William Grier, rode out from Taos to effect a rescue and to inflict some punishment. En route, they picked up the legendary Kit Carson. They tracked the band out to the Canadian River. Carson urged an immediate attack, but Grier wanted to parley. As the Americans hesitated, the Jicarilla were already fleeing. A bullet hit Captain Grier and ended the deliberations. The cavalry charged into the camp, but it was too late. Every Apache but one old woman had vanished into the night. They had left Mrs. White behind, after first firing an arrow into her heart. Before her death, Mrs. White had been reading a thrilling novel featuring Kit Carson and no doubt dreaming of her imminent rescue by that Taos hero. Carson admitted that this episode haunted him particularly; he hated the idea of Mrs. White expecting fictional Kit Carson to rescue her and instead being killed while the real Carson hesitated. Many years later, the Jicarilla admitted to having killed White's child and servant en route since they were slowing down the escape.

IV
AMERICAN BLUES

America Gets Too Close for Comfort

The early years of the nineteenth century saw France, Spain and the newly independent United States of America drawing and redrawing their borders. The sale of Louisiana placed the rebel Americans side-by-side with the royalist Spanish. Paranoia and distrust flared on both sides. Spain prohibited trade with the Americans and jealously guarded geographical information.

The arrival of a group of Americans in 1810 raised red flags as far south as Chihuahua. Although they entered the province west of Taos, the news set everyone abuzz. The Spanish believed that Lieutenant Zebulon Pike and Dr. John Robinson were spies, for many good reasons. They were not exactly prisoners but certainly not free to do as they wished. The Spaniards made every effort to hide cartographic materials from Pike and to conceal their strategic industrial and defensive sites.

Pike stuck to his story about getting lost with his troops, and Robinson stuck to his about trying to collect a debt for a friend. After being "escorted" down to Chihuahua, they were released. Upon their return to the United States, both published extensive descriptions of their treatment. Robinson tried to defect, was rejected as a spy and then really *did* become a spy, then a double agent and, later, a general in the Mexican revolutionary army. His hatred of the royalist New Mexico government and sympathy with the Texan rebels led him to publish extensive manifestos explaining why the

The Sangre de Cristos rising above the Taos Valley. Jane Abrams print from a carving made by Richard Crisler for *Laughing Horse* 15 (March 1928). *CSWR.*

United States should claim all land to the east bank of the Rio Grande. The boundary line he drew on his controversial wall map placed Taos squarely within the lands of American Louisiana.

Robinson died shortly after making his map and after bitterly watching the United States cede the lands of eastern New Mexico to Spain in 1818.

On the other hand, Robinson's Texan friends kept the claim alive for generations. The United States eventually paid Texas for the lands east of the Rio Grande in 1850. Payment took the form of forgiving Texan war debts. Even so, some modern Texan secessionists cite the "theft" of New Mexico among their grievances.

New Mexicans knew what side of the tortilla their beans were on, and they stayed loyal to the Crown and the Church, which so heavily subsidized their colony. During the tumultuous years of the revolution, both citizens and officials tried to distance themselves from the revolutionary Texans, but their real fear was of the Americans. The Protestant Yanquis had recently done terrible things against their king and had very strange ideas.

When Mexico declared independence from Spain in 1821, New Mexico unwillingly became independent as well. The first positive effect of this otherwise unwelcome change was the sudden cession of centuries-old Spanish restrictions on trade across the northern border. When the news reached frontiersman William Becknell, who was crossing the Plains with his wagon train, he abruptly changed course for New Mexico, blazing what would become the Santa Fe Trail. The news of the money that could be made trading in New Mexico soon tantalized a number of traders and trappers who were scouring Louisiana's waterways for the newly fashionable beaver pelts. Taos was the closest town to the new American border, and Taoseños found their valley becoming the de facto headquarters for American trappers.

Mountain Dew of New Mexico

Just as the first priests to arrive in New Mexico planted vineyards for sacramental wine, the first American trappers who settled in Taos built a distillery for taking advantage of the abundant Taos wheat harvests.

Thomas "Peg Leg" Smith was born in 1801 and at the age of twenty-three joined a caravan bound for Santa Fe. He earned his moniker by cutting off his own leg after being shot by an Indian musket. Perhaps the bustle of Santa Fe made him long for the frontier living he had known as a child in Kentucky, for before long he drifted north to Taos. Within a year, he had established his routine of hunting in the Rockies during the fall and spending the rest of the time in Taos, brewing up his signature *aguardiente*.

Peg Leg Smith owned the distillery with three other men, and it proved to be a booming business. Smith was liberal with his stock and livened up many a rendezvous with barrels of his "Taos Lightning." This super-potent brew was approvingly described as making a drinker "knock around like a blind dog in a butcher shop."

Before many years had passed, the demand for Taos Lightning outpaced the supply, even after copycat distilleries opened up throughout the Taos Valley. The quality (such as it was) suffered due to the hasty production required to quench the thirst for these spirits. Lewis Garrard wrote, "Such is the demand, it is imbibed before attaining a very drinkable age, by both foreigners and residents, with great avidity."

The rough plainsmen who drank this hooch so avidly were happy to badmouth the aguardiente, whose name they couldn't properly pronounce. "Makes drunk come mity quick; but t'ain't good—burns up the innards; an' a feller feels like a gut-shot coyote," one critic groused. But whether they called it "Touse arwardenty," "mountain dew of New Mexico" or Taos Lightning, the beverage steadily gained popularity as an export to the booming American frontier towns in Colorado.

In 1858, Uncle Dick Wootton arrived in the newly established town of Denver bright and early on December 25 to brighten the holy day with ten barrels of Taos Lightning. He set nine inside an improvised saloon and carried the tenth in front of a crowd of about two hundred people. While his wife handed out every cup, pot and saucepan they owned, Uncle Dick used an axe to knock in the top of the barrel, hollering that drinks were on the house. Surely no Santa had ever been so warmly received on Christmas morning.

Smith and Wootton weren't the only ones whooping it up with Taos Lightning. French trader Cerain St. Vrain was rumored to have a distillery near his gristmill, which conveniently doubled as a cache for smuggled goods. Around 1830, Simeon Turley built a gristmill and distillery near Arroyo Hondo. The water-powered gristmill produced flour and cornmeal for local consumption. On his looms and spinning wheels, workers created finished woolen goods for trade to California. With his wealth, Turley also built up herds of cattle and sheep for trading to California.

Brothers William and Charles Bent, who also came to Taos about this time, built up a prosperous trade and soon established a fort on the Santa Fe Trail. Bent's Fort on the Arkansas River immediately became a mandatory stopping place for parties of all stripes, including fugitives, trappers, fortune hunters, bands of natives, ciboleros and entire army divisions. Uncle Dick Wootton recognized a similar opportunity on Raton Pass and established the first toll road. Although most Mexicans and Indians tended to just walk around the gate, the Americans appreciated Uncle Dick's entrepreneurial spirit and paid their tolls.

Not all mountain men were such successful businessmen. Old Bill Williams, fabled for wrestling and exterminating bears, tried his hand at retail. Possibly grizzlies seemed easier to cope with than the *señoras* of Taos. Before long, he threw all his trade goods into the street in disgust and returned to roaming the mountains. Long John Dunn (aka Juan Largo de Taos), the eccentric operator of the Taos and Raton stagecoach, came into the princely sum of $500 once but gambled so lavishly that it was gone by morning.

French-Canadian trapper Charles "Don Carlos" Beaubien became partners with Guadalupe Miranda, Governor Manuel Armijo's secretary. The two of them successfully petitioned the governor for a large grant of land northeast of Taos, including part of the mountains and a substantial area of the Plains. This grant caused much muttering in Taos. The law held that people who weren't New Mexican couldn't own land. Beaubien was a naturalized New Mexican, but the Bents were clearly partners in this enterprise. To the vecinos and the natives of Taos, it seemed like Armijo was simply handing land over to the Americans through the back door.

Another early arrival never became rich from his opportunities, but he may have won the best prize of all. Christopher Carson wooed and wed the lovely Josefa Jaramillo, daughter of a prominent Taos family, and together they created a large and mostly happy family. In order to do so, Carson

The house where Kit and Josefa Carson raised their family. *Historic American Buildings Survey; F.D. Nichols, August 1936. HABS NM,28-TAO,2-1.*

turned to the priest who came to the parish the same year Kit Carson arrived on a wagon train—Padre Antonio Martinez. Martinez instructed Carson in the Catholic faith, baptized him and married him to his sweetheart. They celebrated a double wedding with Lucien Bonaparte Maxwell and Luz Beaubien, daughter of land grant owner Charles Beaubien.

Although Taos was the source of a great river of moonshine, the degenerate culture of Santa Fe did not infect the good citizens of Taos. In Santa Fe, "women were bought and sold like horses," but there is no record of any brothel or prostitution in Taos. In Santa Fe, "public gambling was both the leading industry and the leading sport," but even if the people of Taos did regularly wager on cards, dice, roosters, dogs, horses, footraces (as well as anything and everything else), they were genteel enough not to operate public gambling houses.

PADRE MARTINEZ PERPLEXES

Perhaps the citizens of Taos were so circumspect out of their respect for Padre Martinez, who soon influenced every aspect of life in Taos. Born to land baron Don Severino Martinez, Antonio had turned to the priesthood after his wife died. As New Mexico lacked a seminary—or indeed, any institution of higher education—Martinez had to study in Mexico. Being a student during the heady years of the revolution radicalized and inspired Martinez in his work with the impoverished *Nuevo Mexicanos*. It also might have made him too radical for the tastes of the American newcomers.

A number of Americans watched in interest as Martinez consolidated his hold on the hearts and minds of the Taos people. He organized a co-educational primary school (the first in Taos) and a seminary, where he also taught law. He imported New Mexico's first printing press and started churning out a newspaper, *El Crepúsculo de la Libertad* (The Dawn of Liberty), which pulled no punches in calling for reform. He served in the government at many levels.

Padre Martinez also supported a network of Christian brotherhoods in the rural New Mexico villages whose members served their communities as priests, teachers, gravediggers, emergency responders and hospice providers. The *penitente* brotherhood filled the vacuum left by departed missionaries. In independent Mexico, the mission experiment (funded from the king's treasury) came to an abrupt end, and few priests wanted to serve in remote

New Mexico. True to their medieval roots, the penitentes also performed extreme acts of penitence—including self-flagellation and crucifixions—which were proscribed by the Catholic Church and shocking to Americans.

The Americans saw these activities and suspected Martinez of much worse. When his congregation exploded into violent rebellion against the government in 1837, the Americans' suspicions were confirmed.

Assassination and a Coup

A mixed group of genízaro, Pueblo, Apache and Hispanic rebels swooped out of Taos, armed with an anti-tax platform and whatever sharp things they could lay their hands on. They joined more rebels in Santa Cruz. Governor Albino Perez heard of the rebellion and rode to meet them, but his troops defected, so he fled. The rebels rode faster, caught the governor, stabbed him to death, decapitated him and kicked his head around for good measure. For the second time, the Taos people had taken a heavy hand in toppling the government. This time, they took charge.

José Angel Gonzales was also called *El Angelito*, in part for his pleasant nature. His mother was from Taos Pueblo, but his father was a coyote, probably born of a French trapper and a mother from a Plains tribe. His father had been captured as a child and raised by a Spanish family, so José was also raised in this way, leading many to describe him as a genízaro. Like many Taos genízaros, he was a cibolero. Some sneered that being a good shot and excelling with a lance were his only skills. However, he had upwardly mobile dreams and had left the buffalo plains to live in the Hispanic Villa of Santa Cruz.

In hindsight, El Angelito should have continued hunting bison on the grassy prairies. The generalship he received on the field of battle near Santa Cruz and the governor's palace in Santa Fe proved to be his undoing. Former and future governor Manuel Armijo, living in the southern hinterlands near Albuquerque, moved quickly when he heard of the uprising's success. Some alleged that Armijo moved so quickly because he had a hand in toppling Perez himself. Regardless of the depth of his surprise, Armijo assembled his own army of about seven hundred men and began the long march to Santa Fe.

In answer to postmortem accusations, Padre Martinez claimed to have suffered under great pressure from members of his flock to support the rebels. During the initial uprising, the rebels had besieged Padre Martinez's house. Martinez and some prominent citizens had withstood the siege thanks to superior firepower. When the rebels' bows and arrows failed to force compliance, a rebel named Antonio "Coyote" Vigil captured Martinez's brother. Martinez claimed that he finally signed an oath of loyalty to the rebellion only after Coyote Vigil had imprisoned and tortured Santiago.

After El Angelito became Governor Gonzales, Martinez traveled to Santa Fe to bring Gonzales back home. Before they had traveled far, Armijo's army retook the capital. Armijio declared himself governor, but not before writing glowing, heroic accounts of his own bravery to bolster the legitimacy of his self-appointed position back in Mexico City.

Padre Martinez and Governor Gonzales heard the news upon their return to Taos and set out on the road again to confront Armijo's forces. When later confronted with his complicity in the rebellion, Martinez insisted that he was merely fulfilling his duty as the pastor of Taos—when his parishioners were in a battle, he must serve as a chaplain. Indeed, as the two forces met at Pojoaque, Martinez had the opportunity to hear the confessions of many dying men.

Of his own bravery in this engagement, the priest wrote, "[Martinez] deported himself as a brave and charitable soul, hearing the confessions of the wounded and others who died in that action, which duties he discharged with the bullets whistling over his head, and around him, and surrounded by the other horrible apparatuses of war."

The chapel where Padre Martinez held services after his ouster by Archbishop Lamy. *Historic American Buildings Survey; F.D. Nichols, August 1936. HABS NM,28-TAO,3-1.*

When the dust settled, Armijo's forces had captured both Governor Gonzales and his ally, Coyote Vigil. Armijo hanged Vigil for treason and announced that his corpse should be hung on a scaffold, unburied forever, as a deterrent for anyone who might seek to emulate him.

Perhaps thinking of his own tenuous hold on the governorship, Armijo was slightly kinder to Gonzales. As the legend goes, he brought the first indigenous governor to his priest and ordered Martinez to "confess this genizaro, so he can be shot five times." With compassion, Martinez confessed El Angelito, witnessed his execution and buried him at Taos Pueblo.

OCCUPATION AND REBELLION

A decade after Taos erupted in rebellion, the American army arrived to take over New Mexico. Although the army bypassed Taos and occupied Santa Fe without firing a shot, the reverberations shook the residents of the valley. The invaders had appointed Charles Bent as the new governor while they continued to press south to Chihuahua. By this point, Bent had a long and happy history as a citizen of Taos and had a family with Kit Carson's sister-in-law, Maria Ignacia Jaramillo.

Trader and New Mexico governor Charles Bent. *From a portrait in the Charles Bent home in Taos.*

Despite his deep relationships with the people of Taos, they did not celebrate his appointment. The people of the Taos Pueblo were concerned about the land grant that Bent's associate Charles Beaubien had wrangled out of Governor Armijo before the invasion. Most suspected Bent of being a secret partner in the grant and were concerned that access to hunting grounds would become restricted.

The vecinos of Taos were also concerned about what would happen with their lands and their life ways. Despite assurances that the New Mexicans would keep their land and religion, the people were deeply suspicious of what changes this invasion would bring. No doubt, Padre Martinez shared the opinions of other educated New Mexicans that cultural, religious and value system differences would create conflicts and that the impoverished and undereducated New Mexicans were sitting ducks for the land-hungry Anglos.

Their own helplessness to resist, and the shameful surrender of Governor Armijo, made the proud New Mexicans deeply unhappy. Many of them knew of little beyond New Mexico and had been willing to defend their homeland with their lives. Although they had often been the first to benefit from the economic activity generated by the Americans, they preferred it when the Americans were subject to New Mexican laws, with plenty of barriers to prevent them from owning land, marrying their daughters or gaining citizenship.

Governor Bent and Colonel Sterling Price, head of the American troops, quashed one rebellion and scattered the leaders in December 1846. Bent made a speech to a crowd of New Mexicans that he still thought of as "his people," entreating them to be peaceful. He urged them "to remain quiet, attending to your domestic affairs, so that you may enjoy under the law, all the blessings of peace, and by rallying around the government, call attention to the improvements which you deem material to the advancement of the country and that by so doing you may enjoy all the prosperity which your best friend wishes you."

Satisfied with his efforts, he returned to Taos and spent a merry holiday season with his wife and children. Shortly after the New Year of 1847, the governor was relaxing in his home with his family when a mob arrived at his hacienda. Bent tried to reason with the mob but realized it meant business when members fired through the door. He grabbed an axe, cutting through the wall to the next home. Bent's wife enlarged the hole with a poker, enough to creep through. As Maria and the children escaped, the mob broke through the door and filled the governor's face with arrows, hacked at his hands and body, scalped him alive and ultimately decapitated him.

With Governor Bent dead, the crowd moved to purge Americans from the rest of the Taos Valley. The mob sought out Carson and Bent's brother-in-law, Pablo Jaramillo, and drove their lances through his body. The teenaged son of Charles Beaubien hid in some straw with his "Indian slave," but both were betrayed to the mob. One servant in the Beaubien home advised the rebels, who were hesitating over stabbing the cringing boy, "Kill the young ones and they will never be men to trouble us."

After these murders, it was a short step to killing the sheriff, Stephen Lee; the probate judge, Cornelio Vigil; and the circuit attorney, J.W. Leal. Leal suffered the worst treatment at the hands of the maddened men that night. First he was scalped alive, as the governor had been. Once scalped, the men dragged him through the streets behind their horses, pricking him cruelly with their long buffalo lances. After hours of this torture, a "compassionate Mexican" took pity on Leal's pleas for death and shot him.

TURLEY'S BETRAYAL

The rebels were not sated with a clean sweep of the town. The fires spread to nearby Mora, where between four and seven people lost their lives. Two were killed on the Red River. Perhaps the most gruesome battle took place at Simeon Turley's gristmill along the Arroyo Hondo.

Like Governor Bent, Simeon Turley had always considered himself a good friend and neighbor of the New Mexicans. He ground their wheat, brewed their hooch and spun their wool. At first, he felt confident that the uprising would not affect him, but soon it became apparent that he would need to take some defensive measures. Along with seven others—mostly

Skull placed as a warning. *From George D. Brewerton, "Ride with Kit Carson,"* Harper's New Monthly Magazine *(August 1853).*

English, French Canadian and American mountain men—he holed up at his mill and waited for the storm to pass.

When the mob arrived, it demanded total surrender of the mill. Turley refused, so the siege began. The eight inside the mill kept the angry men outside at bay for a full day and night. During the second day, the Taos men managed to sneak close and set the mill on fire. The men inside who weren't already injured or dead tried their best to flee. The crowd fell on the escaping men and killed six. One man hightailed it out as the mob stabbed his friend to death. Turley also managed to escape and ran until he encountered an ally who offered him shelter and a horse. Grateful for this largesse, the terrified Turley waited patiently for his friend to return with help. Instead, his duplicitous benefactor led the mob back to Turley; the mob killed him and then sacked and gutted the mill.

Destruction of San Geronimo

Before the bodies were buried, news of the uprising in Taos had reached Colonel Sterling Price in Santa Fe, who immediately marched on Taos. Soon after, the tragic news reached Governor Bent's brother William at his fort on the Arkansas River. As usual, the fort was full of an odd mixture of voyageurs, ciboleros, sightseers, traders, tribes, trappers and travelers. The news galvanized the Europeans, who swore they would reduce those who scalped Bent to a "heap of wolfmeat."

The trappers at Bent's Fort were hot to lynch everyone in Taos and burn their farms, but the company commander, Captain Jackson, refused to move his troops until he received word from Colonel Price in Santa Fe. Without the support of the army, William Bent assembled twenty-three volunteers, including the old cibolero Manuel Le Fevre, Lucien Maxwell (who would become heir to Beaubien's grant) and several trappers who had followed in Kit Carson's footsteps by marrying Taos belles and were worried about their wives.

As the volunteers on the Arkansas organized themselves and quarreled with Captain Jackson, Colonel Price was already marching on Taos, leading nearly five hundred men and dragging four howitzers. He met the rebels at Embudo and drove them back, chasing them through two feet of snow in the mountains.

The cannons slowed the Americans down enough that by the time the First Cavalry arrived at Taos Pueblo, the rebels had already barricaded themselves inside the Mission of San Geronimo. Steeped in centuries of Catholic tradition, the insurgents felt confident that they had chosen an unassailable position.

To the rebels' shock, the Americans positioned their cannons. Without hesitation, the army began bombarding the church. The heavy cannonballs simply sank into the adobe walls. Soldiers assaulted the walls, and the defenders were able to kill seven, including one Captain Burgwin, who commanded the companies stationed in Albuquerque. Some soldiers managed to climb up to the roof and set it on fire. Others reached the walls and simply started hacking the adobe apart with axes. Wherever they created a breach in the ancient church, the soldiers heaved in a bomb.

General Sterling Price, who crushed the rebellion in Taos. American army portrait. *From* Old Santa Fe, *Vol. 1.*

Far from being a sanctuary, the church had become a death trap. The roof collapsed, and the interior was chokingly congested with smoke. As the rebels fled the burning, exploding church, the Americans shot them down. The Americans captured some, a few escaped and over 150 Mexican and Pueblo fighters died that day.

A TASTE OF AMERICAN JUSTICE

The volunteers from Bent's Fort had arrived the night of the attack, and they could hear the commotion over thirty miles away. They bided their time, gathering up horses, cows and mules that belonged to the Bents or to the army, until Haw-he, an Indian belonging to the Bents, informed them of the rout.

By the time the volunteers came into town, the fighters had been buried, and the leaders of the rebellion were in jail. The governor of Taos Pueblo had been shot in cold blood by a captain of Burgwin's dragoons, John Fitzgerald. "Fitz" was arrested for murder, but an escape was quickly arranged by giving

Ruins of the San Geronimo Mission destroyed in the battle with the American army. *Historic American Buildings Survey; Frederick D. Nichols, August 1936. HABS NM,28-TAOP,1-1.*

him enough firewood to climb up to the window, outside of which waited a horse and a change of clothes.

A "drumhead court-martial" was arranged the very next day. Six men had been captured alive, and a grim Judge Beaubien presided over the trial for treason against the United States. With the death of his young son fresh in his mind, the sentence of "*muerto, muerto, muerto*" was not long in coming. The many observers crammed into the small room did not rejoice. Rather, "the painful stillness that reigned in the courtroom, and the subdued grief manifested by a few bystanders, were noticed not without an inward sympathy."

The irony of being convicted for treason toward an invading country was not lost on American or New Mexican observers. One wrote later, "Justice! Out upon the word, when its distorted meaning is the warrant for murdering those who defend to the last their country and their homes."

Despite the injustice, the execution went forward as scheduled. The contingent from Bent's Fort was pressed into service building a scaffold on Taos Plaza. The men rounded up all the available rope for hanging so many at once and enough soap to lubricate the nooses. Everyone in town showed up to bear witness at the hanging. Fearing more unrest, the army aimed their howitzers at the unhappy crowd.

One of the convicted men offered an impassioned speech before his death. Because he spoke in Spanish, the Americans understood nothing but the last phrase: "*Carajo los Americanos!*" Had his hands not been tied, he probably would have presented his middle finger as well. Despite being bound, two other men grasped each other's hands as they died.

After the dust settled, the Americans were on full alert. Suspiciously, they began accusing Padre Martinez of inciting his flock to rebellion. Martinez and Charles Bent were long known to be enemies. Martinez didn't approve of American encroachment on the common lands of the land grant or the pueblo. Most damning, he had already been implicated as the prime mover behind a gubernatorial coup. As before, the good father strenuously defended himself against such claims. His defense was successful in that nothing was ever proven, but suspicions still smolder 150 years later.

On the other hand, the Americans' distrust of Padre Martinez made the Taoseños love him even more. Support soared for his educational reforms, his community-building efforts and his positions on land grant rights. Thanks to American rumormongering, Martinez expanded his base of followers until he was known—and beloved—throughout northern New Mexico.

More Plots Afoot

The Americans were right that the men of Taos were not finished trying to oust the invaders. Community elders General Jesus Tafoya and Don Antonio Trujillo sent out a circular one year later, instructing recipients to ready their forces and assemble them for an attack on January 22. The instructions concluded, "We have declared war with the American and it is now time that we shall all take our arms in our hands in defense of our abandoned country."

Their plot was detected and halted. The Americans put Trujillo, Tafoya and others on trial for treason in Santa Fe. The dignified men spoke articulately in their defense, pointing out that the Americans had invaded their country, and they were duty bound to defend it. Neither their advanced years or positions of leadership nor their moving testimony was enough to save their lives.

Instead, they suffered the humiliation of being publicly excoriated by the judge before being sentenced to death:

> *Your age and gray hairs have excited the sympathy of both the court and the jury, yet while each and all were not only willing, but anxious that you should have every advantage placed at your disposal that their highly responsible duty under the laws to their country would permit, you have been found guilty of the crime alleged to your charge. It would appear that old age has not brought you wisdom nor purity nor honesty of heart. While holding out the hand of friendship to those whom circumstances have brought to rule over you, you have nourished bitterness and hatred in your heart.*
>
> *You have been found seconding the acts of a band of the most traitorous murderers that ever blackened with the recital of their deeds the annals of history. Not content with the peace and security in which you have lived under the present government, secure in all your personal rights as a citizen, in property, in person and in your religion, you gave your name and influence to measures intended to effect universal murder and pillage, the overthrow of the government and one widespread scene of bloodshed in the land.*
>
> *For such foul crimes an enlightened and liberal jury have been compelled, from the evidence brought before them, and by a sense of their stern but unmistakable duty to find you guilty of treason against the government under which you are a citizen.*
>
> *And there only now remains to the court the painful duty of passing upon you the sentence of the law, which is that you be taken from hence to prison, and there to remain until Friday, the 16th day of April next, and that at two o'clock in the afternoon of that day, you be taken thence to the place of execution and there be hanged by the neck till you are dead, dead, dead! And may the Almighty God have mercy on your soul!*

Theatrical sentencing notwithstanding, the judges in these tribunals were ultimately found to be in error. President Polk wrote of the Americans' trials:

> *It appears that after the territory in question was "in the occupancy of our Army" some of the conquered Mexican inhabitants, who had at first submitted to our authority, broke out in open insurrection, murdering our*

> *soldiers and citizens and committing other atrocious crimes. Some of the principal offenders who were apprehended were tried and condemned by a tribunal invested with civil and criminal jurisdiction, which had been established in the conquered country by the military officer in command. That the offenders deserved the punishment inflicted upon them there is no reason to doubt, and the error in the proceedings against them consisted in designating and describing their crimes as "treason against the United States."*

Thus, the rebels ended up somewhat vindicated in their efforts, although any pardon was much too late to be of help. Apparently, Martinez's views were taken seriously as well. Land grants were specifically protected in the treaty that the United States ultimately signed with Mexico.

TAKING THE JOKE TOO FAR

Martinez remained under suspicion for many years. A new archbishop tried to force changes on Martinez's parish, resulting in a very public fight and Martinez's suspension in 1856, which he ignored. Although the Americans were not particularly affected by this contretemps, they took it as further evidence of Martinez's rebellious and intractable nature.

In 1857, the rumor mill started churning out reports that the priest was conspiring with his brother Pascual to lead another revolt among the New Mexicans of Taos. Kit Carson, who was in town this time, sounded the alarm. Since the original unrest, the army had moved closer to Taos. The soldiers at Cantonment Burgwin, named in memory of the commander who lost his life at the Battle of Taos, were quick to respond. They galloped into town, "hell bent for leather," surrounded the priest's home and interrupted him right in the middle of…sleeping.

Disappointed, but with their adrenaline up, the soldiers spent the night in town. No doubt some enterprising distillery had opened up in the vacuum left by Simeon Turley, and the thirsty soldiers were able to wash the dust out of their throats. The ladies of the town already knew how hungry the men were for biscuits that weren't hard and meat that wasn't wormy. They moved into action and did a brisk trade selling their home-cooked food. Merchants soon realized that bringing the soldiers into town was fantastic for business. No fewer than fifteen false alarms followed in the next few months.

Eventually, the Americans relaxed their vigilance and decommissioned Cantonment Burgwin. Taos was once again a peaceful mountain town. But perhaps the Taos merchants remembered the happy days of the uproars and false alarms. Years later, they had the opportunity to try the same trick.

A miner named John Conway had shot and killed his neighbors, a father and son, over a mining claim. Convicted of first-degree murder, he was sentenced to hang in the Taos Plaza. The local paper, *La Revista de Taos*, published the date far in advance to bring a large crowd from the surrounding communities. On the day of the scheduled hanging, the crowds waited for the big event in vain. Eventually, an official appeared to offer a vague excuse for why the hanging could not proceed that day. The onlookers were left to disperse into the town to eat, shop and drown their disappointment in aguardiente. The tills that the Taos merchants counted that night were full enough that they used this ruse another three times. Each time, *La Revista de Taos* would publish an excuse or correction after the fact.

Who knows how many possible execution dates they might have scheduled? *La Revista de Taos* did not publish the final date. As the story is told, Conway eventually slit his own throat with a sharpened spoon. The doctor was called in to stitch him up so he could be hanged sometime in the future, but the effort was futile. A deceased Conway was hanged with no ceremony and no spectators.

V
LAWYERS, GUNS AND LAND

Under the Treaty of Guadalupe Hidalgo, "legitimate titles to every description of property personal and real, existing in the ceded territories, are those which were legitimate titles under the Mexican law in California and New Mexico." American lawyers and land speculators immediately understood that if they could define what "legitimate title" was, a lot of money could be made.

Las Cruces lawyer and New Mexico senator Albert Bacon Fall gained notoriety for allegedly accepting bribes in the Teapot Dome scandal but had a corrupt reputation before that. *Library of Congress Prints and Photographs Division, Harris & Ewing Collection.*

Some of the lawyers who came to the newly created New Mexico Territory, like Stephen Elkins and Thomas Catron, had known one another back East. No matter where they came from, they formed a tight friendship in New Mexico and worked together at every level of the courts and the territorial legislature. Some became judges, some became governors and some became senators. The press dubbed this group the "Santa Fe Ring," but their reach extended to every square acre of New Mexico.

FLOWERS WILL NOT BLOOM FOR YOU

The attorneys of the Santa Fe Ring had their own particular style of entertainment. Circuit judge Kirby Benedict was particularly famous for the gallows humor of his pronouncements (as well as for his gambling and drinking). Attorney General William Breeden recorded one sentence that Benedict passed on Jose Maria Martin of Taos, who was convicted of aggravated murder without provocation. After deliberating, Benedict said:

> *Jose Maria Martin, stand up. You have been indicted, tried, and convicted by a jury of your countrymen of the crime of murder, and the court is now about to pass upon you the dread sentence of the law.*
>
> *As a usual thing, Jose Maria Martin, it is a painful duty of the judge of a court of justice to pronounce upon a human being the sentence of death. There is something horrible about it and the mind naturally revolts from the performance of such a duty.*
>
> *Happily, however, your case is relieved of all such unpleasant features. The court takes a positive delight in sentencing you to death. You are a young man, Jose Maria Martin, apparently of good constitution and robust health. Ordinarily you might have looked forward to many years of life, and the court has no doubt you have, and expected to die at a green old age, but you are about to be cut off in consequence of your own act.*
>
> *Jose Maria Martin, it is now the spring-time. In a little while the grass will be springing up green in these beautiful valleys and these broad mesas and on the mountain sides. Flowers will be blooming, birds will be singing their sweet carols and nature will be putting on her most attractive robes, and life will be pleasant and men will want to stay.*
>
> *But none of this for you, Jose Maria Martin. The flowers will not bloom for you, Jose Maria Martin. The birds will not sing their sweet carols for you, Jose Maria Martin. When these things come to gladden the senses of man, you will occupy a space six by two beneath the sod, and the grass and these beautiful flowers will be green growing about your lowly head.*
>
> *The sentence of the court is that you be taken from this place to the county jail. That you be safely kept and securely confined in the custody of the sheriff until the day appointed for your execution.*
>
> *Be very careful, Mr. Sheriff, that he have no opportunity to escape, and that you have him at the appointed place, at the appointed time. That you be so kept, Jose Maria Martin, until—Mr. Clerk, upon what day of the month does Friday about two weeks from this time come?*

> *"March 22d, your honor."*
>
> *Very well, until Friday, the 22d of March, when you will be taken by the sheriff from your place of confinement to some safe and convenient spot within the county, and that you be there hanged by the neck until dead.*
>
> *And the court was about to add, Jose Maria Martin, "may God have mercy on your soul," but they will not assume the responsibility of asking an All Wise Providence to do that which a jury of your peers have refused to do. The Lord could not have mercy on your soul. However, if you affect any religious belief, or if you are connected with any religious organization, it might be well for you to send for your priest or your minister and get from him, well, such consolation as you can, but the court advises you to place no reliance on anything of that kind.*

Breeden relates that Jose Maria Martin did indeed escape the county jail and the noose and lived peacefully for many years before falling out of a wagon and breaking his neck. Charles Bent's daughter refuted the legend and claimed that Martin was executed on schedule and buried in an unmarked grave in the Taos cemetery.

THE DEADLY ROAD TO ELIZABETHTOWN

Unlike the swift justice of the district courts, the land grant courts moved slowly, so the people of Taos escaped the lawyers' clutches for a time. Meanwhile, a gold strike in the mountains drew a different kind of speculator. Shortly after a rich lode was discovered in 1866, the community of Elizabethtown sprang up. Funded by investments from the Taos upper crust, including Illinois-born Lucien Maxwell, hundreds of miners were soon tunneling into the Sangre de Cristos. Along with the miners came thousands of saloon operators, gamblers, prostitutes, gunfighters, preachers and an assortment of con men, drifters and lost souls. The epitaph of Elizabethtown's one-time sheriff, Clay Allison, explains that he "never killed a man who didn't need killing." Allison was a notorious Texas gunfighter who once killed a man as they ate dinner together.

Traffic between "E'town" and Don Fernando de Taos was fairly steady. One immigrant set up a sort of inn near the summit of Flechado Pass between the towns. The *Hispaños* called him Carlos Cañada, but the Anglos called him Charles Kennedy. All agreed that he was a burly man with "bulging blue eyes and coarse red hair." Somehow he wooed and wed the pretty Gregorina Martinez, an acculturated Ute. Soon she had a baby, and the couple seemed happy enough.

The road was dangerous. Often a miner would set out from Elizabethtown and never reach Taos, disappearing without a trace. The Kennedys were having a hard time, and guests often gossiped about their fights. One day, Mrs. Kennedy came running down the road toward a group of travelers, sobbing for help. Charles Kennedy had thrown their baby into the fire.

The men rode to the inn and demanded an explanation from Kennedy. He admitted to killing the baby and then surprisingly admitted to killing thirty-one guests. He and his wife had been fighting because she had to bury all the bodies, and he finally lost patience with her and killed their child. He

Elizabethtown threatened to eclipse Taos in importance. John Collier, photographer. *Library of Congress, Prints & Photographs Division, FSA-OWI Collection.*

led the men to many graves, some of which held multiple corpses, although they did not recover all those slain.

Kennedy was taken to prison in Elizabethtown, but he was not to remain there for long. Led by Clay Allison, the Elizabethtown vigilantes pulled him from his cell and lynched him. Allison laid claim to the head and strung it up outside a popular Cimarron bar, the St. James Hotel, where it hung for a long time.

Despite the best efforts of Clay Allison, Charles Kennedy and the like, E'town kept growing. At one point, the population reached five thousand citizens and supported several newspapers. Quite a few of these migrants gazed at the vast expanses of New Mexico and dreamed of becoming land barons. Anglos preferred Elizabethtown, where they could create their own society, separate from the established order in Taos.

ELIZABETHTOWN AND LAND WARS

Unfortunately for the town's growth, Elizabethtown encroached on private land. When Governor Armijo granted Guadalupe Miranda and Charles Beaubien their lands in northeastern New Mexico, he included a terribly vague description of the boundaries. As part of their evaluation of the Mexican land grants, the Americans surveyed the grant (now owned entirely by Lucien Maxwell and his father-in-law) and found that the acreage exceeded one million square acres, which seemed to abut the burgeoning town of Elizabethtown and completely encompass Cimarron.

Lucien Maxwell was an easy-going guy and well liked by both the Anglo and Hispanic communities. He had a stake in the growth of Elizabethtown and wasn't going to rain on the parade by being a stickler about fences. Nor was he troublesome about collecting rent from the hundreds of squatters who were pouring in from every direction. The land grant courts were a different matter and well worth his attention; they claimed that his grant was too large and began contesting the title. In order to simplify matters, Maxwell bought out Guadalupe Miranda, who had since moved to Mexico.

Before long, Maxwell had had enough of the collections, the squabbling and the courts. He sold the grant to three men, including Colorado senator Jerome Chaffee, who turned around and sold it to an English syndicate, which created the Maxwell Land Grant and Railway Company. The English owners hired some New Mexicans to be their representatives. These four turned out to be members of the Santa Fe Ring, and soon the land wars were on.

One of the primary movers behind the Maxwell Land Grant and Railway Company was Stephen Elkins. He served as the territory's attorney general, as U.S. district attorney and as territorial delegate to Congress. Elkins worked closely with his brother-in-law and college friend Thomas Catron to exert their influence on Congress, judges, surveyors and local politicians to gain every advantage in their land deals. Together, they rewrote the law where they could and bent the rules where they couldn't.

Rand McNally "Auto Trails" highway map, 1925. *Image No: 5566001 Rumsey Collection.*

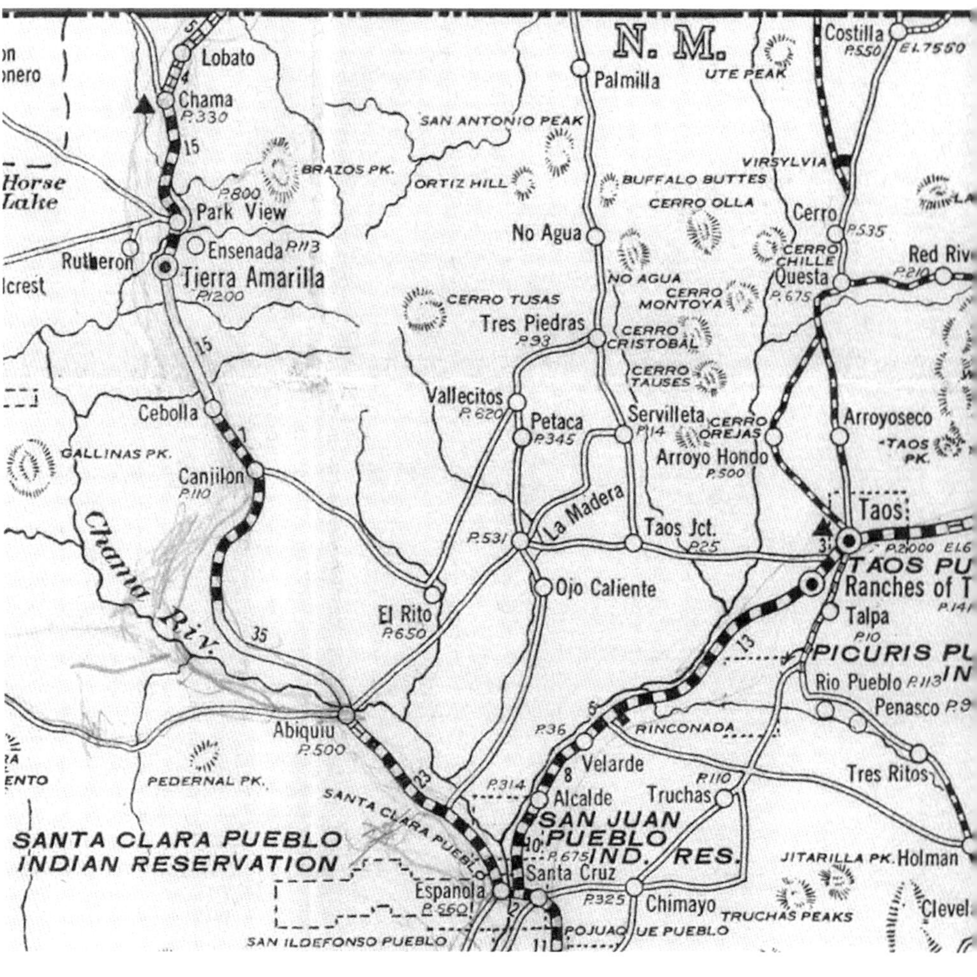

The Maxwell Company (as represented by Elkins and the Santa Fe Ring) started trying to evict the hundreds of squatters. Instead, it roused the rabble's ire. Parson F.J. Tolby, a minister from Colfax County, made his name speaking against the company. He wrote letters to newspapers all over the country condemning corrupt New Mexico politics and corrupt New Mexico politicians, specifically the Santa Fe Ring. The popular preacher was murdered on the road to Elizabethtown in the fall of 1874—allegedly—by the ring's hirelings.

A Civil War veteran named Cruz Vega was blamed for the murder. Clay Allison was probably the leader of the mob that lynched Vega and hanged him from a telegraph pole near Cimarron. Two days later, it was Allison who shot Pancho Griego, Vega's partner, in retaliation for Tolby's death. Even prominent citizens were swept up in the mayhem. Attorney Melvin

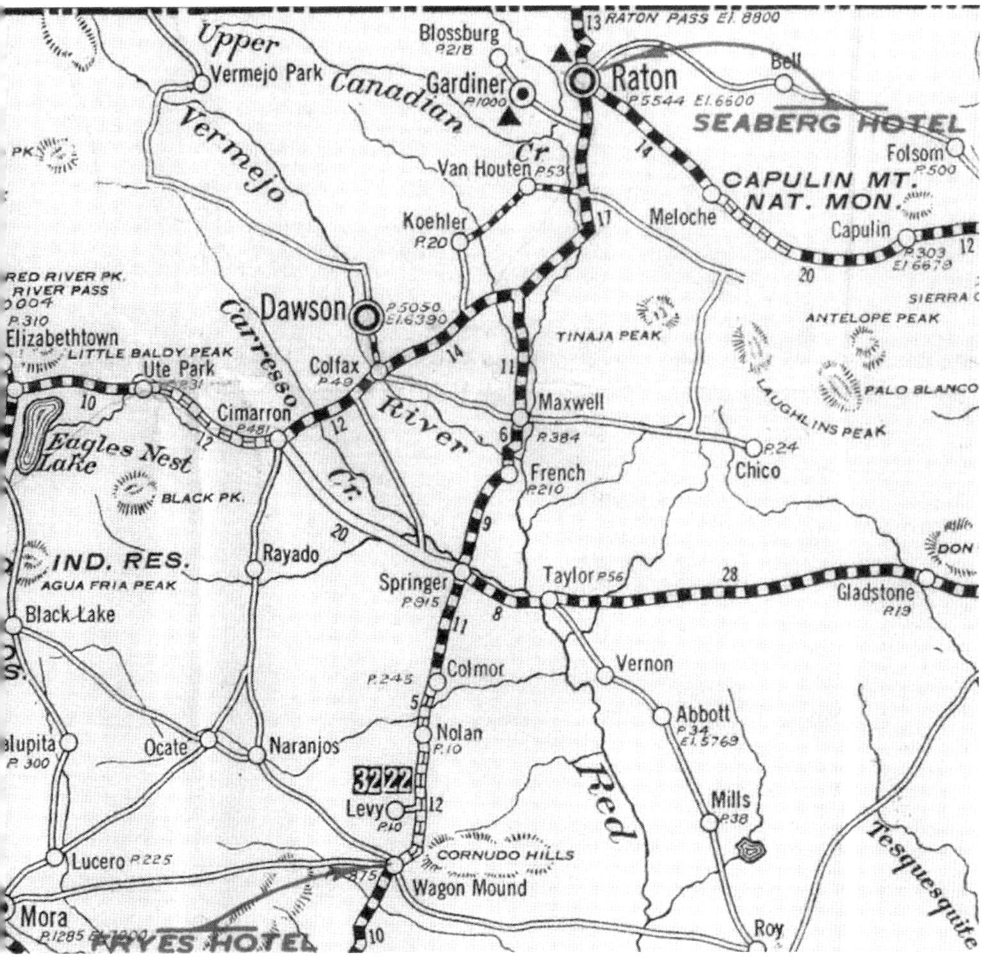

Mills was arrested for being the paymaster behind Vega's hit on Tolby, and the governor (Sam Axtell, a Ring member) had to send the cavalry from Fort Union to release Mills before the lynch mob arrived. A doctor suspected of being part of the ring barely escaped ahead of a crowd of angry squatters.

After the primary targets of the anti-grant faction were out of the way, the mobs went after anything they could. People burned houses and pastures of their neighbors who held opposing views. Cattle were rustled by the score. More than two hundred people lost their lives.

The Colfax County War, as it came to be known, was bad for the business of the Maxwell Land Grant and Railway Company. Under pressure to resolve the situation, Ring member Governor Axtell pushed a measure through the legislature that ended up heaping fuel on the fire. The legislation permitted the company to demand rent from the squatters and established a grand jury in Taos to adjudicate any disputes originating in Colfax County, where most of the grant lay. The settlers on the land grant didn't want to have to fight their battles in Taos and reacted furiously. To them, it was just another instance of the Santa Fe Ring protecting their own interests at the expense of the little guy.

"The fighting parson" Oscar McMains had stepped into the shoes of the murdered Tolby. He encouraged the settlers to refuse to pay rent and kept the wars simmering long enough that the Maxwell Land Grant and Railway Company went into foreclosure. The Ring scrambled for new investors and found some in Holland who willingly set up the Maxwell Land Grant Company with Stephen Elkins as president.

Some allege that Santa Fe Ring member Senator Stephen Benton Elkins ran for Congress solely to patent the massive Maxwell Land Grant. *Library of Congress Prints and Photographs Division.*

New owners and a new name made no difference. The squatters refused to pay rent, and the natives who considered this land part of their domain escalated their attacks. McMains continued to keep the rabble fired up. In frustration, Elkins ran for Congress, became a senator and deftly maneuvered the Supreme Court into ruling favorably on the title for the Maxwell Land Grant.

In 1887, the title was cleared and the war was over. The squatters who had lost their homes slowly drifted away.

By then, the E'town gold mines had long run out. Only a few dozen people remained of the thousands who once thronged there. When a fire swept through in 1903, burning most of the remaining structures, the lingering residents began to abandon Elizabethtown. The last mine closed in 1917.

MANBY'S MACHINATIONS

Despite the machinations of the American lawyers of the Santa Fe Ring, one of the most unscrupulous land dealers in Taos was an Englishman, Arthur Rochford Manby. In 1883, Manby crossed the ocean to settle on the Maxwell Land Grant with his brothers. Within a year, the Manby men were embroiled in a dispute with their neighbor, Dan Griffin, that ended in a fatal shooting. Arthur took the blame for killing Griffin, and a judge in Raton accepted his claim of self-defense.

Perhaps wanting to get on the good side of the pro-grant thugs, Manby signed up with a territorial militia led by Bat Masterson's little brother James. The militia was disbanded as quickly as it was formed, and the angry militiamen decided to let off steam in Raton. Manby probably rode with the mob as they cursed, shot out windows, smacked down citizens and threatened bystanders with their guns. A number of men were prosecuted for hooliganism, but Manby escaped arrest.

If Manby had hoped to curry favor with the land grant company, his efforts were in vain. In 1891, he was evicted along with everyone else. Displaced and angry, he washed up in Cimarron but quickly left after killing a man in the St. James Hotel. The man had been pacing outside Manby's room and had tried the knob. Manby listened until the man started to walk away and then stealthily opened the door and shot the stranger several times in the back.

After this incident, Manby turned his sights to Taos, still dreaming of acquiring a grant of his own. Upon moving to Taos, he learned of the Martinez land grant. Don Severino's heirs had been dividing the land since his death in 1827, and each case was grinding slowly through the process of surveying and validation in the land grant court.

Manby saw his chance. He was consumed with the prospect of becoming the owner of the Martinez Land Grant, smaller but far richer than the arid highlands of the Maxwell Grant. The Rio Grande

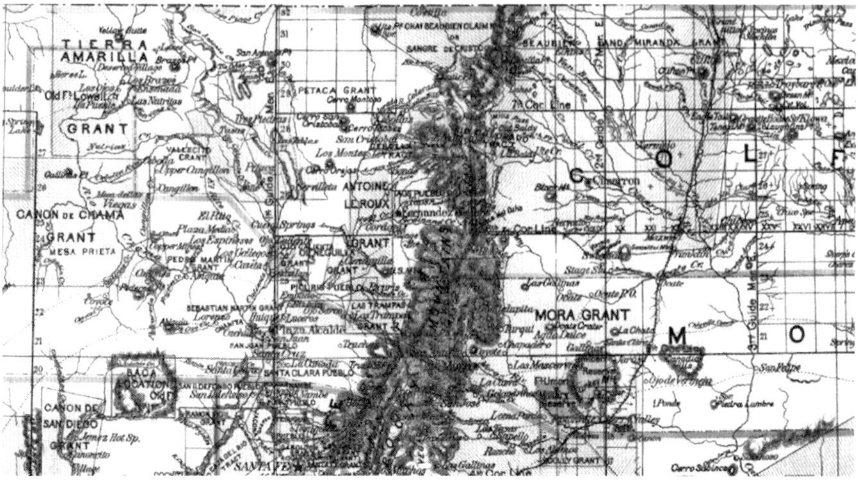

Land grants in the territory of New Mexico, 1879. Although the Beaubien Miranda Grant fell mostly in Colfax County, Taos County was given jurisdiction over all claims. *U.S. General Land Office map.*

bordered the Martinez land Grant to the west. Lower Taos Canyon formed the southern border. On the east, the grant lands brushed the town of Taos, skirted around the lands of Taos Pueblo and then stretched up the slopes of Wheeler Peak before ending at the source of the Rio Hondo, which formed the northern border. This treasure included water, arable lands, timber, hot springs, and possibly even mineral-rich deposits. After surveying the Martinez Grant, Manby couldn't wait to get his hands on it.

First, he needed money. He traveled back to England and talked the ears off several investors about his glorious prospect. Meeting with mediocre results, Manby returned to Taos. Over the next two decades, Manby's patter, prospectus and charm would become polished enough to lure several English and American investors into his scheme.

Meanwhile, Manby turned to the mines around Elizabethtown for capital. There, he befriended the wily Columbus Ferguson and his sweet young daughter, Terecita. Ferguson and Manby held the Mystic Mine and the Ajax Mine in partnership with a third man, Frank Wilkerson. William Stone had been Ferguson and Wilkerson's partner, but he died mysteriously after Manby showed up. Gossips wagged about Stone's death, weighing both Wilkerson and Manby as potential suspects, but nothing ever came of it.

Many thought that Stone was killed when he objected to the partners' new business strategy of high-grading ore. The criminal ring pilfered ore from the most productive mine in the region, the Aztec, and then stored

Pueblo Revival–style adobe house. Jane Abrams print. *CSWR*.

it in the played-out Ajax. Pretending that the Ajax was still producing, the partners could ship the stolen ore at seemly intervals.

From these highly illegal operations, Manby soon acquired enough money to start buying up parcels from the many heirs of Severino Martinez. He built a rambling nineteen-room hacienda on Pueblo Road and worked with a young Pueblo man named Tony Lujan to plant trees, turning the approach to his estate into a gracious boulevard.

As his partners were toiling away in Elizabethtown, Manby was improving his mind. He managed the books for the mining business and feverishly studied land grant law. He penned terrifying letters to landowners, convincing them that unscrupulous men were after their land but that he could save them. Manby then proceeded to fleece every one of these poor farming families.

In 1905, Manby formed the Taos Valley Land Company and put a sympathetic Raton judge (and Santa Fe Ring member) on the board. Then he embarked on another fundraising tour. Investors in England and Chicago were much more impressed this time and showered Manby with money and promises of more money. On returning to Taos, Manby prudently took a large chunk of this money and put attorney Charles Catron, son of the legendary Thomas, on retainer.

Together, Catron and Manby pulled off coup after coup in the courtroom and behind the scenes. In some deals, Manby was able to snatch up prime parcels for pennies on the dollar by getting the value of the land reduced and then buying the land for taxes. In other cases, he bamboozled landowners into signing their deeds over to him in the belief that it would protect them from the new American laws. Few of the essentially illiterate New Mexicans or the frontier lawyers could match his knowledge or tenacity. A favorite tactic was to snow understaffed courts with an endless flow of petitions, challenges, writs, suits and bills. One investigator later noted that Manby knew more "than five other lawyers combined."

For a single year, a Mrs. Manby presided over this growing estate. Edith Kellogg Prescott was the sheltered daughter of some of Manby's investors. The enchantment she initially felt for her husband soon wore off, and she fled back east. Neighbors described her as "a pink-nosed little rabbit mesmerized by a boa constrictor."

After Edith left, Arthur Manby entered a frenzy of paper shuffling. He formed the Taos Land Company, the Colonial and Security Company, the Taos Irrigation Company, the Mesa Irrigation Land Company and the Taos Valley Fruit Company. Each of these corporations served as a shell for other corporations, and he juggled money among them to fund his ongoing land purchases, court costs and attorney fees.

This empire—although monumental only on paper—was expensive, and Manby needed ever more money. He wrote heaps of letters to potential investors. He spent years trying to hawk a "Van Eyck" painting he owned. Arthur Manby did not shy away from selling his charms in a more direct manner. One of the rich women he romanced with his suave British manners and enthusiasm was the heiress Margaret Waddell, who gave him money for several years.

Manby worked a particularly cruel con on the patriarch Don Juan de los Reyes Santistevan. Manby had befriended the family and led them to believe he was interested in marrying one of their daughters. As he might approach his son-in-law, Don Juan approached Manby to apprise him of the family's dire financial straits. Manby convinced Don Juan that the best course was to hand over the family's assets to Manby so that they could declare bankruptcy. As Don Juan worked through his end of the deal, Manby set up shell corporations that appraised and bought the Santistevan land at a low value. When the appraisal was challenged, the friendly judge Napoleon Bonaparte Laughlin (who served on the Taos Valley Land Company Board) ruled in favor of Manby. With the favorable ruling in hand, Manby callously evicted the whole family from their ancestral home. As a follow up, he sued them for court fees—payable, of course, in more land.

Although he wooed many rich women in his life, Manby's true love was the daughter of his partner, Columbus Ferguson. Little Terecita had grown into a lovely woman but was still considerably younger than Manby.

The older man was passionately devoted to Terecita, and she returned his interest until it became clear he would never marry her or share his fortune with her (although Manby did buy her a trailer court in Taos). Despite this, they continued a stormy, sometimes romantic, often criminal relationship until his death. Like her father, Terecita did not shy away from illegal means of personal enrichment, including extortion and a variety of other scams.

By 1913, Manby had put all the pieces of the puzzle in place to own the Martinez Land Grant. He had twisted arms, lied, conned and committed fraud, but his day of victory was close at hand. All that was left was the court decision, and Manby's legal expertise served him well. The court decided to patent the entire Martinez Land Grant to Arthur Rochford Manby.

Manby held the land for three years before it all fell apart. Investors started suing him for fraud. The territorial government came after him for taxes due. Lawyers started picking apart the complex web of companies he had established and pruning away his empire. By 1917, nearly the entire estate had been auctioned off for debt. Manby was left nearly destitute, with only his house and the surrounding twenty-three acres of land.

BURSUM BILL AND BAD COMMISSIONER BURKE

The players of the Santa Fe Ring hadn't stopped their machinations. In 1922, ring members Senator Holm O. Bursum, Secretary of Interior Albert B. Fall, attorney Ralph Twitchell and A.B. Renehan cooked up a doozy of a land bill. Senate Bill 3855 would give U.S. courts jurisdiction over Pueblo land claims. Inimical state courts would adjudicate land and water claims. Worse, the bill defined the boundaries of pueblo land according to the "Joy Survey," which mapped all claims against pueblo land, not the actual boundaries.

No matter how you looked at it, the impacts of such a bill on the pueblos would be catastrophic. Taos alone would have lost four thousand acres of its sixty-thousand-acre grant. Any trespasser or squatter would suddenly have a legitimate claim, and the pueblos would have absolutely no recourse or compensation.

But by this time, some influential Anglos had settled in Taos, and led by socialite Mabel Dodge Luhan, they soon threw their weight behind opposition to the Bursum Bill. John Collier wrote an article for the *World* called "Robbing the Pueblo Indians." Alice Corbin Henderson wrote "The Death of the Pueblos" for the *New Republic*. Elsie Clews Parsons wrote an article called "Ku-Klux-Klanned" but was

Pueblo governors Santiago Naranjo, Waihusing, James Miller and Jesus Baca, each wearing a blanket and carrying a cane given to him by Abraham Lincoln as a token of promise of permanent retention of their lands. The men were in Washington, D.C., to protest the Bursum Bill. *1923 Underwood & Underwood photograph courtesy of Library of Congress Prints and Photographs Division.*

unable to find a publisher. Artists, writers and anthropologists joined the protest, including Ernest Blumenschein, Mary Austin, Willa Cather, Hamlin Garland, John Sloan, Harriet Monroe, Edgar Lee Hewett, Witter Bynner and D.H. Lawrence. Sponsors even financed a trip of Pueblo governors to Washington, D.C.; New York City; and Chicago. There, John Collier spoke against the Bursum Bill, the governors held dances and the media soaked it up eagerly.

Furious, Secretary Albert Fall denounced the articles and speeches as "propaganda." He described the protest as "insidious, untruthful, malicious, and even criminal libel." Nonetheless, the Bursum Bill was defeated, thanks to popular outcry. Fall himself would gain permanent notoriety a year later when he had to resign from his position after he was accused of taking bribes in the (wholly unrelated) Teapot Dome scandal.

Hydra-like, the Anglo need to settle the land grant claims sprouted new legislation in place of the axed Bursum Bill. The substitute bill would establish a commission to settle pueblo land disputes "in a manner as fair to the Indian as to the white settlers & squatters," as Mabel Luhan described it. Her ceaseless stream of letters alerted a network already organized for battle. In defense of the new bill, Indian commissioner Charles H. Burke entered the fray.

Almost immediately, Commissioner Burke got into a contretemps with the ladies of the Indian Welfare Committee of the General Federation of Women's Clubs. After he presented an overview of the new legislation, Committee chair Stella Atwood told him that his policies were "inhumane, expensive to the tax-payer and largely fruitless of good to the Indians."

He told her to mind her own business. Warming to his theme, he added that the Indian Bureau would tolerate no further meddling from the ladies of the Indian Welfare Committee. Mrs. Atwood caustically reminded the commissioner that "he was the servant, not the master of the American people, and that the Indians did not belong to him as his private property."

Burke was out for blood. On Easter Sunday, he showed up at Taos Pueblo to issue an order in person: the Taos people must put a stop to all their ceremonies at once. As Mabel Luhan wrote to Elsie Parsons, "What a stupidly cruel thing to do." Burke didn't let up, and the vigilant Luhan reported his every move in her letters as her husband, Tony, passed on the news.

After Fall's resignation, Burke dragged the new secretary of the interior into a meeting of Taos Pueblo's council. In the meeting, Burke told the assembled men that they were "half animals" because of their "pagan worship." Mabel commented, "Another case of American bullying, of the hundred percent variety."

On the heels of the widely debated Bursum Bill, eastern newspapers were quick to pick up on the new scandal. For comment, the *New York Times* approached Burke, who (perhaps unknowingly) echoed the hated pre-revolt missionaries. Burke supported his ban by asserting that the "dances take up too much time, that they interfere with work, and that they are evil and foolish."

This callousness was too much for the pro-Pueblo contingent to bear. They swiftly organized to drive Burke out of office. In their demands for Burke's resignation, they echoed Mabel's sentiment: "It is not merely a silly order, as the *World* calls it…it is a criminal order."

Indian commissioner Charles H. Burke. *Library of Congress Prints and Photographs Division.*

Franklin Roosevelt replaced Burke with John Collier, the capable man who first sounded the alarm about Senator Bursum's dirty bill. Burke himself had a personal vendetta against Collier and accused him of "subverting the Indians, and of organizing them against the government." It must have been a bitter pill to cede his office to this rabble-rouser.

BATTLE OVER BLUE LAKE

Despite the best efforts of the well-meaning Anglos in New Mexico, Taos Pueblo did not get all the land grant acreage it deserved and required. Shenanigans in the surveyor general's office led to dubious surveys, as well as to common lands being stripped from grants. In the case of Taos, the surveyor general stripped many of the lands on the upper Rio Pueblo watershed, including its source, Blue Lake.

It is hard to describe the critical role that Blue Lake plays in the spiritual life of the Taos Pueblo. The lake—believed to be a place of emergence from previous worlds—is so sacred that the Taos people are reluctant even to talk much about it, except in general terms. The annual pilgrimages to return to the lake were long hidden from anthropologists, and the secrets of the ceremonies, particularly those conducted lakeside, were not to be discussed on pain of death.

A Taos governor in the 1950s tried to draw analogies that the Anglos could understand:

> *Blue Lake is the most important of all our shrines because it is part of our life, it is our Indian church, we go there for good reason, like any other people would go to their denomination and like a shrine in Italy where the capital of the Roman Catholics worship is different: people go visit and give their humble words to God in any language that they speak. It is the same principle at the Blue Lake, we go over there and talk to our Great Spirit in our own language and talk to Nature and what is going to grow, and ask God Almighty, like anyone else would do.*

Despite the fact that Blue Lake was absolutely essential to the well-being of the Taos people, Theodore Roosevelt made it part of the National Forest System in 1906 and transferred ownership to the Carson National Forest upon its designation in 1908. It took awhile for the pueblo to hear the news and understand the implications. In 1912, the tribe appealed to the commissioner of Indian Affairs. The commissioner approached the secretary of agriculture about returning the parcel but was flatly refused. The tribe continued to find a way to reclaim the land where they had lived since the time of the cottonwoods.

The Pueblos' case came before the Pueblo Lands Board, established in 1924 to settle land disputes. The board agreed that the tribe should not have lost the land and awarded it munificent compensation for the lake and the surrounding area. Frustrated, the elders offered to relinquish any money due them if only

Jim Barnes, a surveyor with the New Deal–era New Mexico Reassessment Survey. *1941 photo by Irving Rusinow for the Department of Agriculture, Bureau of Agricultural Economics. NARA record: 5307166.*

they could regain title to their land. Ultimately, the Pueblo Lands Board gave them neither compensation nor title.

When the erstwhile John Collier became the commissioner of Indian Affairs, he was able to persuade the secretary of the interior to adopt his point of view. In the end, the secretary of the interior agreed to bring the lands under federal control so that Indian Affairs could control the "improper and immoral" ceremonies that the Taos were rumored to conduct during their pilgrimages to the lake. Not knowing what really happened led to rampant speculation, and tongues wagged that the girls looked particularly "wilted" upon their return.

With the Department of the Interior and the Bureau of Indian Affairs behind the movement, the matter came up for discussion before the Senate Indian Affairs Committee in 1933. The Senate agreed that title should be restored. Instead, the Department of Agriculture delayed doing anything for seven years while protests mounted. Finally, Taos Pueblo got a special "native use rights" permit. The tribe could have exclusive use of the corridor for its annual ceremony and full access at any time.

Perhaps a native use rights permit would have been good enough had the Forest Service been the kind of steward of the land that the Pueblo had been. Instead, the rangers stocked the lake with non-native fish and then allowed fishing with dynamite. The prayer sticks and sacred oars left by the devout were regularly cleared away, while trash, bottles and fishing wire proliferated. Logging operations left scars in the surrounding forest and filled the once-quiet air with the sounds of machines.

The Taos people continued to protest to Congress. Finally, they turned the tide by using First Amendment arguments. In 1965, the Pueblo and their supporters managed to get a bill introduced to Congress that would protect the tribe's freedom to worship at their "church." Some congressmen firmly opposed the measure, fearing the precedent such a bill would set. Indeed, many tribes that had lost sacred lands watched the case closely.

The Taos Pueblos' Paul Bernal testified before Congress in 1969. The revered late leader explained why the Taos didn't trust the Forest Service with Blue Lake:

> *In all of its programs the Forest Service proclaims the supremacy of man over nature; we find this viewpoint contradictory to the realities of the natural world and to the nature of conservation. Our tradition and our religion require people to adapt their lives and activities to our natural surroundings so that men and nature mutually support the life common to both. The idea that man must subdue nature and bend its processes to his purposes is repugnant to our people.*

The hippies who were flooding into Taos about this time appreciated this philosophy and picked up the cause. As the Taos artists had done a generation earlier, the Anglo counterculturalists networked with their friends across the country to generate national interest in and support for the Taos Pueblo. Sixty-four years after the lands were stripped from the tribe, a landmark decision returned the sacred Blue Lake to Taos Pueblo in 1970. Today, the lake is closed to the public, to protect both the watershed and the Pueblo's religious ceremonies.

VI

SCANDALOUS BOHEMIANS

A Fresh Start for Mrs. Sterne

A broken wagon stranded two artists in Taos in 1898 and inspired them to start an art colony in the little town. The Taos Society of Artists remained a genteel club of romantic artists like founders Ernest Blumenschein and Irving Couse for several decades. They happily painted dreamy landscapes, handsome Indians and rugged cowboys.

When the rich and restless Mabel Dodge Sterne visited in 1918, the collegial boys' club had no idea of the storm that was about to break on their shores. Mabel was visiting with her third husband, Maurice. Her first husband, a steamship heir, had died in a hunting accident. She separated from her second husband, a wealthy architect, after seven years of marriage. Five years later, she married the temperamental sculptor Maurice Sterne, despite the objections of her family.

In an effort to inspire Sterne, the couple traveled to Taos, but Mabel was the one who found inspiration. Mostly, her inspiration seemed to stem from her fascination with Tony Lujan, a Taos Pueblo man who played tour guide to the Sternes. By the end of their visit, Maurice was itching to return to New York City, and Mabel was itching for him to go. After some bitter debates, Maurice returned east, and his wife stayed to began building her empire in Taos, with Tony Lujan at her side—that is, as much as his wife, Candelaria, would allow.

Mabel had been deeply dissatisfied and restless back east. In New York, she cultivated artists, writers, intellectuals and radicals, but her friends' great ideas failed to inspire her. Her many husbands and her lover—the family doctor—not only disappointed her romantically but also infected her with a venereal disease. Young Mabel was waiting for her lover when he arrived in clear discomfort. "That damned bitch of Dr. Sherman's has given me the clap," he complained. Mabel wrote, "Feeling puzzled, but noble, I cried, 'Give it to me and I will take it for you,' and throwing himself passionately upon me, he did so."

Dr. John Parmenter, a gynecologist who was providing end-of-life care for her father, not only gave her gonorrhea but also added insult to injury by carrying on with Mabel's mother at the same time. Confronting her mother and Dr. Parmenter only got Mabel exiled to Europe for being a pest.

In Taos with Tony, she made a fresh start. Mabel and Maurice had rented part of Arthur Manby's rambling hacienda, now sadly decrepit. After Maurice left, Mabel turned her energy to buying land and constructing a new house with Tony's invaluable assistance. The next task was filling her house with friends and sympathetic characters. Mabel was an inveterate writer her whole life. As a wealthy woman, her time was her own, and she spent much of it filling endless journals and firing off countless letters to a global circle of witty and talented friends.

"That's enough bacon, Spud." Mabel rushes to stop Spud Johnson, while Mary Austin cooks at the stove and Tony enters through the door. Jane Abrams print of a carving by Gina Knee for *Laughing Horse* 20 (Summer 1938). *CSWR*.

With her rambling estate, sharp ear for gossip and vast inheritance, Mabel was in a prime position to pluck glorious artists, musicians, writers and thinkers from the rarified salons of the East and replant them in Taos. The lists of Mabel's guests are endless but would be incomplete without mention of Aldous Huxley, Leopold Stokowski and Georgia O'Keeffe. In the case of O'Keeffe, her life was indubitably transformed by New Mexico, but it should be noted that she maintained a decorous distance from Taos after one season living with Mabel…and spending far too much time alone with Tony. In this way, Mabel Dodge Luhan (who changed the spelling of her name to assist her Anglo friends) became the center of every story about the transformation of Taos from a sleepy frontier town to an exclusive capital of arts and culture.

THE LAWRENCES PLUS ONE

D.H. Lawrence in his passport photo.

Mabel's excited missives about her "discovery" of Taos reached writer D.H. Lawrence and his wife, the Baroness Frieda von Richthofen. The Lawrences had their own reasons for dissatisfaction and an entirely different set of martial woes. D.H. Lawrence considered himself a radical free thinker whose aim was to free himself from the bonds of convention. In his book *Women in Love*, he describes his protagonist (closely modeled after himself): "What it was in him he did not know, but the thought of love, marriage, and children and a life lived together in the horrible privacy of domestic and connubial satisfaction, was repulsive…The hot and narrow intimacy between man and wife was abhorrent."

Lawrence did ultimately marry Frieda, although she was already married when they met, with a staid professorial husband and three rosy children. When she fell in love with her husband's student, he encouraged her to turn her back on her bourgeois home and middle-class family. Frieda did, though not without a miserable backward glance for her children.

She was granted her divorce (but not custody of the children) in 1914, but the new couple was not to know happiness in chaste and war-torn Britain. Lawrence's book *The Rainbow* earned him serious enemies and no end of legal trouble. The book was suppressed after an obscenity investigation. Frieda was accused of being a German spy. They suffered in terrible poverty, grinding out books that no publisher would touch due to Lawrence's tarnished reputation, not to mention the First World War.

As soon as they could, the Lawrences fled Britain. They traveled through Italy, Germany and Austria. Like Mabel, Lawrence drew from a deep well of dissatisfaction. Nothing in bleak, postwar Europe could satisfy the void in him. He began to imagine a utopia of right-thinking intellectuals and enthused endlessly about the perfect society.

Lawrence found at least one passionate adherent to his cause. Bloomsbury artist Dorothy Brett, the bohemian daughter of Lord Esher, was utterly smitten by Lawrence and ready to follow him to the ends of the earth. When Lawrence read Mabel's letter, he and Frieda agreed that if there was nothing for them in Europe or New York, America's Wild West might hold what they were looking for. By this time, Lawrence (and particularly Frieda) had tired of Brett's fervent adoration and clinginess. The Lawrences' first visit to Taos was as a couple, but when they returned for a longer stay, the unshakeable Brett was at their side.

Brett had suffered a similar crush on writer John Middleton Murry but had refrained from acting on it until his wife, Katherine Mansfield, expired from tuberculosis. At long last, Brett gave full voice to her longing for Murry. He was amenable about consummating their long friendship but, in short order, became overwhelmed with her attentions. He pushed her to a distance, and when she persisted, he fled the country. For the rest of his life, Murry needed only to crook his finger to bring Brett running to his side, but for the most part, he chose to keep her far away. After the grief over Murry's rejection abated, the devoted Brett transferred her boundless veneration to the gaunt, bearded and cynical Lawrence.

The Lawrences were indeed entranced, charmed, moved and changed by Taos, as was the Honorable Brett. Mabel hosted them lavishly and soon fell under the spell of Lawrence's charms herself. Despite her husband's disdain for "connubial satisfaction" and her own adulterous past, Frieda was jealous and bitterly possessive of her husband. Lawrence's dreams of communal living soon died, never to be resurrected.

Within a few months, the tension in Mabel's house became too much to bear. At Lawrence's request, Mabel offered them a small cabin in the mountains, and Frieda happily packed their bags. Her joy was tempered when she realized that Brett was still forming an awkward spoke in their wheel. Lawrence defended her presence because he needed her typing services, so Frieda reluctantly continued to tolerate her. Breaks to go into town and visit the Luhans were hardly a relief, with alpha dogs Frieda and Mabel snarling at each other.

By spring, the Lawrences could take no more. They left for Mexico, replacing Brett with the dapper Spud Johnson and his older lover Witter Bynner, of Santa Fe. D.H. Lawrence never lived much in Taos again. When he did, he employed Spud Johnson as his secretary rather than Brett. For her part, Brett stayed on the ranch and continued her battle with Frieda by post for several years. Many petty squabbles stemmed from the handling and disposition of the assets the Lawrences had left behind—the ranch and the manuscripts that Brett had typed.

Brett, who never saw much commercial success with her paintings, spent her whole life trying to scrape together enough money to live on. When she became too poor, she would move in with Mabel, initiating a flurry of penned complaints about Brett from Mabel to Frieda and responding showers of gripes about Brett in response. At one point, Brett actually did sell some of Lawrence's manuscripts but vehemently claimed that they had been given to her as payment. Despite her grinding poverty, Brett's love for Lawrence was overriding; she never sold another manuscript and eventually surrendered them all to Frieda—after a typically bitter fight.

Lawrence was sick with tuberculosis, and Brett was anxious to spend more time with him. He continued to roam and returned to Europe, where he and Frieda quarreled. Lawrence sent for Brett, and she gladly begged enough money from her friends and noble relatives to fly to her beloved's side. In Europe, Lawrence changed his mind about having Brett near and fled in advance of her approach. He rejoined Frieda, but they soon parted—again. Brett finally caught up with Lawrence, and they spent several idyllic weeks hiking and painting together. She breathlessly drank in every pearl of wisdom from his lips and committed every stormy glance to golden memory.

Finally, Lawrence told her that he had to have sex with her in order to continue their friendship. As always, Brett was happy to give Lawrence what he wanted. Unhappily, the writer was not up to the task and finally blamed the lady. "Your pubes are all wrong," he snapped irritably before leaving the sobbing Brett "ashamed, bewildered, miserable." Brett returned to Taos to nurse shining recollections of her hero for the rest of her days.

Bust of D.H. Lawrence. Jane Abrams print of carving by Ida Rauh for *Laughing Horse* 13 (April 1926). *CSWR.*

Lawrence and Frieda got back together, although another lover—Angelo Ravagli, who was to leave his own wife for Frieda—hovered in the background. When Lawrence died in a French sanatorium, Frieda at first interred him nearby. Word arrived that both Brett and Mabel were hard at work on their memoirs in Taos, and Frieda decided she had to be on the scene to salvage Lawrence's memory. She enlisted Ravagli (who accepted an allowance from Frieda to leave his wife) to help her return to Taos, with the eventual goal of bringing Lawrence to rest there.

Perhaps distance had also dimmed Frieda's memory of how irritating Taos could be with Mabel and Brett around. Tempers flared almost immediately. Brett was horrified that Frieda had brought her lover along and claimed to be "more truly [Lawrence's] widow than Frieda." At a party to welcome the couple, Ravagli started a flirtation with Mabel.

The plan to reinter Lawrence in Taos also ran afoul of the deep rivalries among the three women. Four years after his death, Frieda finally managed to bring her husband's ashes back to Taos, only to learn that Mabel was cooking up her own plans for the remains. Unexpectedly, Brett had joined forces with Mabel, and together they had enlisted quite a few friends to their cause.

In order to preempt whatever anyone else might plan for her husband, Frieda mixed Lawrence's ashes with mortar and poured the entire mess into a little altar she and Ravagli had built. Not even Brett and Mabel—two of the most tenacious women Taos has ever seen—could steal Lawrence after that.

Over time, the conflicts that separated the women diminished, and they treasured one another's company until their deaths. After a life of penury,

Mabel Luhan, Frieda Lawrence and Dorothy Brett, Taos's legendary femmes fatales. *Cady Wells photograph, courtesy of Yale University Beineke Library.*

Brett's exquisite painting of Taos ceremonials finally became popular, and she lived to instruct a generation of hippies about Taos culture. At the age of seventy-one, Frieda finally married her lover of twenty years, and they had six years of marital bliss before she died in Taos, on her seventy-seventh birthday.

MARITAL MISERIES

Although Mabel Luhan once scoffed at Lawrence for being a "typical lower middle class, puritanical conventional englishman; a mass of taboos & prohibitions, inferiority & mother complexes, not to mention the Jehovah complex," she had her own neurotic dark side. Stealing Tony Lujan from his wife turned into a singular act of defiance against society. In New Mexico, she was known as the "woman who married an Indian." But as a woman of independent means living in a society of her own creation, Mabel shrugged off most criticism. What irked her were the people who coveted her husband, just as she had coveted him when he was married to another.

Among her friends, the handsome and exotic Tony aroused much admiration, and numerous were the artists who urged him to pose, the visitors who begged him to drive them to the sights and the many women who sought his attentions in a thousand small ways. The madness of his married life rarely ruffled Tony, but he did suffer for marrying an Anglo.

As a man of the Taos Pueblo, Tony was stripped of his ceremonial positions. He had to pay his ex-wife Candelaria a monthly allowance, and many of her relatives harbored resentment toward him. Although Tony worked hard to maintain his ties with his relations, clan members and friends in the pueblo, he became more and more of an outsider. Anthropologists in Mabel's circle published secret information, and Tony got blamed for leaking the knowledge.

Although Mabel and Tony's love was legendary and her public devotion to him blameless, there is evidence in her journals that she stopped having sex with him early in their marriage. Tony had enjoyed a liaison with a friend's wife in the pueblo and carelessly wiped himself off with his white *manta*, the characteristic blanket of the Taos men. When Mabel detected the stains, she also noticed a telltale discoloration and odor. Having already had two syphilitic husbands, Mabel was quick to recognize the signs of infection. Sure enough, both Tony and Mabel had syphilis. Perhaps Mabel had transmitted it from one husband to another, but she certainly blamed Tony, both for the casual infidelity and the disease. She wrote dolefully, "Three times and out. The third husband who had syphilis, all of them dignified and rather eminent men in their various situations. Is it possible there is so much venereal disease in the world?"

Dr. Thomas "Doc" Martin, the local doctor, was a terrible gossip, so at first Mabel insisted on seeking treatment in Santa Fe. Eventually, they did accept treatment from Doc Martin, who pronounced them both cured after several months of dangerous, painful and expensive treatments. Around this time, Mabel also talked Tony into undergoing radiation treatment for some nodules in his throat, which destroyed his vocal cords. He confessed to his wife, "When I am in my ceremonies or out with the boys singing and I can't sing no more I feel like cryin'. Hurts me inside." Mabel admitted that her husband's greatest pleasures were "singing and loving," but despite the loss of the former, she was adamant about refusing the latter. She claimed to have never made love with her husband again.

Mabel tried to be understanding when Tony sought in others what she denied him, but more often, she intimidated, shamed and annoyed other women, like Georgia O'Keeffe, into keeping their distance. Some women

"Well I guess I can eat a can of sardines." Portrait of Mabel and Tony Luhan. Jane Abrams print of a carving by Gina Knee. *CSWR.*

proved more challenging to keep away. Millicent Rogers proved to be the most challenging of all.

The gorgeous, frail heiress was already in her mid-forties when she blew into town. She had already enjoyed three husbands, as well as lovers who included Roald Dahl, Clark Gable, Ian Fleming and several European royals. Ill from childhood rheumatic fever, drinking hard but still as lovely as a film star, she quickly gained sympathy from many in town, but Mabel's enchantment with the newcomer soon wore off.

Millicent Rogers developed a passion for Native American art and quickly set out to build her collection, which grew to several thousand artifacts. She enlisted Tony to help her meet craftspeople and spent lavishly on their outings. Mabel writhed with suspicion but kept silent, hoping Millicent would soon leave New Mexico.

Instead, Millicent bought her own home and started building her collection in earnest, even developing her own jewelry designs. At the same time, she drew the most interesting people of Taos into her circle, setting herself up as a direct rival. Mabel drew her husband back to her by requiring the construction of a new (and final) house because Millicent had "poisoned" her other house.

Millicent soon acquired the affections of Tony's young nephew as well. The young and handsome Benito Suazo became Millicent's driver, lover and drinking partner. Mabel fretted over the bad influence of the older woman on her husband's nephew. For her part, Millicent delighted in needling Mabel by referring to Benito as her "grandson." Mabel self-righteously denounced Millicent's drinking, even though it was the only lubricant that could allow the two women to meet in public. Mabel was particularly irritated that Rogers would serve alcohol at the Indian dances she hosted; Mabel served nothing stronger than juice to dancers at her house. She also criticized the gifts that the Standard Oil heiress would shower on the people of Taos, dressing the men in silk shirts and fur-lined coats.

In private, Mabel struggled with herself. She knew that Tony was lonely for female company. She wrote:

> *Can I help feeling it is less suffering for me to see him have a little fun with Millicent, than to feel lonesome, knowing he is away some where with her…and if only this old fashioned possessiveness about him would die and cease tormenting me so I could love him purely and unselfishly and really be glad for him!*

In the end, she settled on confronting Rogers. She wrote, "Whether Tony & you continue to see each other is up to him; naturally I cannot do anything about that. You can see him at your house, or before at Manuel Suazo's house…or anywhere else. But not here…I have too deep a distrust of you to be happy with you."

As Mabel was seriously considering divorce, Tony showed up with a bloody, bandaged head. Benito and Millicent had been drinking hard, and he crashed her car. Mabel relented about seeking a divorce, and she and

"The sun is overhead, and the earth is underfoot." Tony is eating, Brett is seated at the table, Mabel is singing at left and Mary Austin is to the right of the table. Jane Abrams print of a carving by Gina Knee for *Laughing Horse* 20 (Summer 1938). *CSWR.*

Tony struggled along, furnishing their new house. One night, Millicent Rogers hosted a huge party with a bonfire, but it started raining, so the group repaired to Brett's house. Everyone got terribly drunk on the lavishly flowing whiskey, and Benito flipped the car on the way home. He was pinned under it and had to be hospitalized for broken ribs. This was the wake-up call that Tony needed to stop straying. Benito recovered and remained devoted to Millicent Rogers until her death.

Once Tony was home again, Mabel found it easier to endure blows like the journalist who wrote of Rogers, "She has become the social arbiter of this well-known artists' colony, usurping the position hitherto held by the aging Mabel Dodge Luhan." Mabel had a quiet chuckle when she discovered that Brett had attached herself to Millicent's household and made her Jamaica vacation quite miserable by irritating and antagonizing Benito.

If Millicent had been healthier, she and Mabel could have duked it out for years. Sadly, she fell ill in 1952 and spent most of the last year of her life bedridden. Benito was utterly devastated by losing his love, and Mabel generously opened her home for him to heal his grief. Sometimes living longer is the best revenge.

FORBIDDEN KNOWLEDGE

Many of Mabel's dearest friends shared her passion for the Pueblo culture. Some applied their artistic talents to interpreting Taos Pueblo, and some applied their scientific techniques. The former were tolerated, but the latter's enthusiasm for uncovering deep and sacred secrets came into direct conflict with the social mores of Pueblo society. One writer commented, "United States government representatives, and missionaries are bad enough, from the Indian's point of view, but they are more tolerable than journalists and, above all, ethnographers!"

An earlier anthropologist had already poisoned the well to a certain degree. Matilda Cox Stevenson studied the pueblo in the early 1900s. She was consumed with curiosity about the annual Blue Lake pilgrimage and ceremony and pushed until she was allowed to witness certain parts of the ritual. Immediately, she published a monograph detailing every secret the Taos had hidden from the world for centuries. The Taos, who had been suspicious of Stevenson to begin with, were furious at the betrayal and swore to keep their secrets more secure. Edward Curtis noted that a man at San Ildefonso was actually executed for working with her.

The incoming Anglos felt no compunction about freely violating the boundaries placed by both the Hispanic and native communities. Many rich easterners in Taos would make parties to spy on the penitente ceremonies around Easter. The processions included fascinating dirges, flagellation, self-torture and crucifixion, plus mysterious business that happened out of view, indoors, prompting wild speculation among the Anglos. Sometimes the spies were caught and sent home under guard. One man convinced the *hermanos* to allow photography and then violated their trust by publishing pictures and lurid descriptions of the holy ritual.

Taos penitentes strap their hooded brother to the cross in an annual reenactment of the crucifixion. Jane Abrams print of a carving by Manville Chapman for the *New Mexico Sentinel*, April 1939. *CSWR.*

Elsie Clews Parsons, another daughter of an eastern millionaire, came west in pursuit of these exciting anthropological studies. Like Mabel, she quickly shed her husband in order to pursue her own interests. Parsons spent years working with people from many different pueblos, including Acoma, Zuni and San Ildefonso. Periodically, she would return to Mabel's house and work on her relationship with the Taos. By 1922, she felt that she was ready to begin research in earnest.

The Taos people warned her against asking questions. One informant told her, "People want to find out about this pueblo; but they can't. Our ways would lose their power if they were known, just as Zuñi ways and the ways of other places have lost their power." Parsons shrugged off the "obsession of danger from giving information." She wrote of interviews with two informants, "I was presented daily with a vision of death from giving information." She wrote rather breathlessly to a colleague how she expected that anyone working with her would be "severely punished, if not executed."

At Santa Clara, she interviewed a man who believed he had nothing else to lose after several family members died because they told "some white person something." Any situation might provide a sympathetic and attentive observer like Parsons with clues to the secret, sacred life of the pueblo, and she proceeded with great patience to collect pieces of the puzzle.

She hired many people from the pueblo to do work around her property and engaged her workers in seemingly casual conversation. At first, she used her knowledge of the practices at other pueblos to ask questions. As she learned more about the clan structure and internal politics, she was able to leverage existing schisms among clans to reveal closely held information. Informants often wept when they realized the extent of the knowledge Parsons accumulated, but she persisted. One of her informants became pregnant and worried about suffering a difficult pregnancy.

As she "cleaned out" one informant after another, word spread that Parsons was starting to know too much. In response, she made it widely known that her writing would never "get back to Washington." She ignored the point that this knowledge was severely proscribed, even from other Taos people. In order to mask her intentions, she was very careful not to reveal the existence of her many publications on Pueblo culture.

As resistance continued to build, Parsons tapped her fortune and started to spread more hard cash around. Even with millions to draw from, she was hardly lavish. She recorded one hard-nosed negotiation with a Taos woman. Parsons was compiling a list of the kivas and needed it checked. No one should have had this information, and the woman was terrified.

She demanded, "How much will you pay for my fear?"

Parsons offered a dollar.

The woman sniffed, "I would not tell you that for one dollar!"

The heiress answered, "Don't be greedy!" to which the woman answered that she wasn't greedy, but she expected the transaction to kill her, in which case she wanted to enjoy a silk dress before her demise.

Ultimately, the implacable ethnologist pieced together a fairly vivid picture of the sacred interior life of the pueblo. From the East, pressure mounted to publish this groundbreaking research. She dithered over her manuscript and wrote a lavish *apologia* absolving any individual from the crime of revealing secrets. Finally, she sent her paper off to Yale University for publication as part of the General Series in Anthropology. In her contract, she stipulated that the book should never be available in New Mexico. Then, particularly worried for Tony Lujan (who was already suspected of being too friendly with the Anglos), she dedicated her book to him. Cautiously, she wrote, "To my best friend in Taos, the most scrupulous Pueblo Indian of my acquaintance, who told me nothing about the pueblo and who never will tell any white person anything his people would not have him tell, which is nothing."

Worried that even these measures were insufficient, she enclosed a note in each copy of the book that said, "We would greatly appreciate an effort on your part to keep this paper from getting into the hands of people in and around Taos. It may cause conflict in the pueblo and create difficulties for future ethnographic investigations there."

This strategy worked for about two years, until a New Deal employee working with the Taos happened to mention the monograph. All hell broke loose. The elders sent for a copy of the book and for two interpreters to translate it.

According to Mabel, who wrote to her anxious friend about the fallout, the interpreters spent "nine days and nights" carefully reading the entire book to the assembled council, and as a result, the Taos were "raising Cain" and "simply wild." Some felt their fury would be best vented by hiring a lawyer to sue Parsons for libel. Others suggested that they would be justified to "kill someone over this."

As a result of Parsons's research, people in the pueblo learned things about each other they were forbidden from knowing. The workings of the clans, moieties and *kivas* are not to be freely shared, but Parsons had apparently done a rigorous job, and now everyone knew everything—that is, everything but whose loose lips were threatening to sink this ship.

The council launched an investigation straightaway to find out who had "come out from under his blanket" by talking too much. Knowing of Parsons's riches, each member's financial records were the first objects of scrutiny. Her servants were interviewed at length to learn whom she had hired and how frequently. As people fell under suspicion and were cut off from the social and economic life of their community, they mailed surreptitious pleas for help to their benefactress. She waved off their problems, assured them that it would blow over and offered the dubious comfort that perhaps the furor was simply the result of a bad translation.

Warming to this theme, Parsons wrote some furious letters to the Office of Indian Affairs for sending inadequate translators and for not heeding her warning about the monograph. She wrote to Mabel, asking her to calm everyone down because she hadn't written about anything important, just gossip. Mabel replied tartly that calm was out of the question: "They are bent on tracking the traitors down if it takes forever—the penalty will be unguessable—maybe death—you can see what storm is raging."

The ethnologist seemed strangely blind to the depth and scope of the anger toward her. Now she decided that the way to resolve this brouhaha was to sit down with all her Pueblo friends and talk the whole thing over amicably. Mabel dutifully passed along this suggestion to the son of the man who was suing Parsons for libel. "I asked Luis…why wouldn't it be a good thing for Dr. Elsie Parsons to come and visit the Indians and have some talks and try and clear it up and he replied gently, 'I am afraid we will have to scalp her.'"

The investigation and prosecutions were wrapped up by 1941. Parsons's primary informant had indeed died after talking to her, so the council determined to prosecute his son instead. He was divested of his share of pueblo lands, his affiliation with his tribe, his water rights and his family honor. Others suffered to a lesser extent. The entire pueblo renewed its wariness toward anthropologists, and few studies have been allowed since then; those that are permitted are on strictly predefined topics.

Mysterious Murder in the Mansion

During the time the wealthy bohemians were reimagining the village of Taos, Arthur Manby had suffered many reversals. Since the glorious day when he had bamboozled enough New Mexicans to gain title of the entire Martinez Land Grant, he had been reduced to paupery. His love affair with "Princess Terecita" Ferguson soured slowly. For a while, they ran a petty extortion ring together, the Turquoise Hill Gang, but she eventually pushed him out in favor of a new lover, closer to her age.

Deprived of even his criminal income, the impecunious Manby was forced to rent rooms to Mrs. Mabel Sterne and her husband, Maurice, but this intimacy was unbearable for all concerned. The soon-to-be-divorced Mrs. Sterne laughed at her mad landlord and tormented him gently. His tenants' strange behavior made Manby all the more crazy. Perhaps Mabel would have been more sympathetic had she known that Manby, along with approximately 12 percent of the Taos Pueblo, was suffering from syphilis, and its symptoms induced extreme paranoia. Manby became more and more reclusive, guarding himself with large and vicious dogs.

In 1929, neighbors became slowly aware that Manby had vanished. His home was tightly locked and barricaded, so the sheriff had to break in. Inside one locked room, he found a rotted, decapitated corpse and Manby's police dogs. In another room, he found a disfigured head, unidentifiable due to the fact that the flesh on the right side of the face was missing.

At first, shocked neighbors presumed that Manby had fallen ill and been savagely torn apart by his own dogs. A verdict of death by natural causes was read. The sympathetic townsfolk chipped in for a respectful burial, as the "rich miser" Manby was unaccountably without a penny to his name.

Crazy enough to shoot a rat. Jane Abrams print of a carving by Jack Clayworth for *El Crepúsculo*, November 1950. *CSWR*.

Nobody could think of anything nice to say about the deceased, except that "he planted the trees in this park and on pueblo road."

However, Manby was still British, and the embassy launched an investigation. Starting with an exhumation, the detective learned that the head had been separated from the body by a saw, not by teeth. Furthermore, the grounds for verifying the corpse as Manby's were slight. As these revelations shook the town, rumors started flying.

No one had believed that Manby was really as impoverished as he seemed. He must have had gold from his mines socked away somewhere. Hadn't he killed one of his mining partners? Travelers reported seeing Manby alive and well in Mexico and in Britain. Soon, many were convinced that Manby had murdered a man in order to fake his own death and start a new life elsewhere.

Others turned their sharp tongues on Terecita Ferguson and her new husband, who were under indictment for a string of robberies, arson and looting. In their minds, there was no other logical conclusion to such a long and wholly inappropriate affair.

The long and thorough investigative report discounted all the eager speculation. Sadly, relying on solid evidence did not clarify whether Manby was a murderer or whether he was murdered. Without any idea of what kind of crime was committed, it was impossible to identify the other party (or parties). Whoever it was got reinterred under Manby's tombstone, and there the mystery rests today.

VII

LOS HIPPIES

I went downtown, what did I see? Hippies, hippies, one, two, three.
—*Taos children's song*

In 1967, some members of the counterculture movement established the New Buffalo Commune in Arroyo Hondo. Enthusiastic dropouts from suburban American culture flocked to the Sangre de Cristos to make the scene. Before long, communes were springing up everywhere. In addition to New Buffalo, seekers could join Five Star, Reality Construction Company, Morningstar, the Lama Foundation or The Family. The Hog Farm and others nestled in the mountains southeast of Peñasco. To the north, another cluster of communes lay near the Spanish Peaks. The hippies who floated from Libre or Drop City in Colorado south to Taos may not have known that they were following trails laid by centuries of hunters, but they might have "dug it."

The Taos newcomers hoped their communities would realize ideals of self-expression, pacificism, tolerance and disdain for the material world. Idealists saw a blank slate in Taos—an opportunity to create a new society. Few appreciated that Taos already had a society, one steeped in conservative Catholic values.

Ritual observances united the Taoseños in different ways throughout the year, from dances at the Pueblo to fiestas in the town. Many Hispanic men still participated in the rigorous observances of their penitente forefathers, though no longer in public. Both Pueblo and Hispanic residents lived by

"There is an old rooster, a tough bird." Raising pet goats and chickens has long been a hobby for the well-heeled of Taos, while others need their chickens for food. Jane Abrams print of a carving by Frieda Lawrence of her favorite rooster for *Laughing Horse* 21 (December 1939). *CSWR*.

the same moral code, and most understood the rules without being told (although elders were always happy to remind mischief makers).

The hippies didn't understand the rules, spurring countless complaints among the traditional residents. The women dressed immodestly and didn't keep their children clean. Many men sported long hair and acted silly. Hippies weren't ashamed to loaf and receive charity rather than work hard for a living. Worst of all, hippies were all irreverent Communists.

The truth was that if you hung out in bars with hippies, you might end up with a lecture on Marxist principles. Some lectures on common property might have been dull, but one man from Guadalupita's Kingdom of Heaven commune actually burned a fistful of money for punctuation. The astonished crowd of impoverished ranchers snapped. Men seized the four hippies in the bar and hustled them out to a quiet place. They raped the woman repeatedly and pistol-whipped all three men until they could barely move.

The terrified victims returned to their commune to recover, only to have their assailants show up again the following day. As the adults fled, the Taos men started shooting. One man was hit in the back and killed. The assailants never came to justice, and before long, the Kingdom of Heaven fell apart.

Many of the hippies were trying hard to live by nonviolent principles, so the local men would viciously bait the hippies in the hopes of getting a rise out of them. It was never long before the verbal taunting would turn to punching. Some hippies responded by giving as good as they got, but more were badly beaten and injured.

A sign of the times. *Courtesy Travis Simon via Creative Commons.*

The Taos hippies, dedicated to a path of nonviolence, were at first loathe to fight back and instead turned to the authorities. But the authorities didn't want the hippies around either. No witnesses seemed to notice the savage public beatings in broad daylight. Law enforcement rarely bothered to investigate incidents like vehicles and buildings getting shot up or even dynamited. Anonymous phone calls to communes threatening arson and murder received little more than raised eyebrows, although when arson was committed, the police would pay a visit and shake everyone down for drugs. One hitchhiking longhair landed in the Taos jail for a "concealed weapon"—a pocketknife.

Many Taos merchants barred hippies as patrons. Some went further. One sign appeared: "The only good hippie is a dead hippie. Kill." In response, the hippie community established its own businesses, such as a macrobiotic restaurant. Someone torched it. The Family, an open-marriage commune, opened a school, a free clinic and a "visitor center" for the incoming flood of dreamers. The school windows were shot out.

Some left in response to the violence. The Reality Construction Company, west of Arroyo Hondo, armed its members. Men from The Family became hyper defensive, maintaining obsessive patrols and radio communications. Hunkering down was good for those who were serious about building a sustainable life because they had time to build, farm, tend to their animals and sell candles, jewelry and other crafts. The others explored the boundaries of their freedom by throwing loud, wild parties; gardening naked; and skinny-dipping in the local hot springs.

Seeking a Family

A teenager named Linda Drouin was one of the first commune residents of Taos, ostensibly seeking God but really fleeing an abusive stepfather. She drifted away, but too poor to make it on her own, she drifted back just as broke as when she left. However, now she had a husband, Bob Kasabian. Linda played as an organist around town and entertained at area bars. Bob and Linda had a baby, but the little family fell apart quickly. Bob and baby Tanya headed east, and Linda went west to Los Angeles, where she felt that she and Bob could start afresh. The family was reunited until Linda became pregnant again, and Bob left her—again. Single, pregnant and with a toddler in tow, she fell into the loving arms of Charles Manson's Family, who offered lavish care and love in exchange for total loyalty.

A year later, Linda Kasabian returned to Taos alone and sought out her friend Joseph Sage. Sage, a Zen Buddhist monk who wandered from commune to commune in a bus, was happy to see his prematurely gray-haired friend but sorry to see her so agitated. She explained that she had come back for custody of her daughter, who had been placed in foster care. The kindly monk willingly engaged an attorney for her and helped her recover her daughter. But Linda Kasabian was still miserable. She finally confessed to Sage that she had participated in some homicides with other Family members, although she hadn't personally killed anyone. She described helping to cut phone lines with the other women, while the men shot a resident coming out of the home.

Sage quizzed her disbelievingly for a while and then made her call Manson's Spahn Ranch for confirmation. The woman on the other end, Patricia Krenwinkel (known to the Manson Family as "Katie"), confirmed to Sage that Linda was crazy and that she fabricated stories all the time to seek attention. She then asked to speak to Linda. "You just couldn't wait to open your big mouth, could you?" she spat. However, the trusting Sage believed Krenwinkel's story and supplied his prevaricating friend with money for the road.

What the good monk didn't realize was that sweet Linda was in way over her head and involved in a string of robberies and homicides. As the only Family member with a valid driver's license, she was present at most of the "creepy crawls" that funded the Manson followers' lifestyle. The scene she described to Sage didn't come close to revealing the full horror of the gruesome murders she helped commit in August 1969. Watching from a distance as your friends murdered a stranger seemed sanitary compared to the truth of the screams, blood and the fear of saying no to Manson.

When the police finally caught up to Linda Kasabian, she was happy to testify as chief witness for the prosecution in return for full immunity. The ever-loyal Family members mocked her tears at the crime scene photographs and tried to paint her as the real mastermind behind the murders. Thanks to Linda's testimony, Manson and four followers were duly convicted and imprisoned.

Kasabian stayed in the western commune life for a while but eventually obtained a divorce from Bob, took her children back east, remarried and settled down to a quiet, private life. The Secret Service watched her closely through 1976, but by then it was clear that Linda Kasabian had finally found the peaceful life she first sought in Taos over a decade before.

How Low You Go to Get High

At first, Taos citizens felt that they had a handle on the hippie problem, but in 1969, the movie *Easy Rider*, featuring the New Buffalo commune, hit the theaters. So many impressionable young people watched the movie and headed to Taos that residents recall that summer not as the summer of love but as the "summer of the hippie invasion." *Easy Rider* star Dennis Hopper himself fell in love with Taos and purchased Mabel Luhan's estate within the year.

Hopper followed in the great doyenne's footsteps insofar as he invited all sorts of luminaries to Taos while he edited his concept film, *The Last Movie*. But luminaries in 1970 didn't comport themselves with the same dignity as Mabel's guests. Hopper himself was consuming vast quantities of alcohol and cocaine, and his guests, like Janis Joplin and poet Richard Brautigan, were also legendarily intoxicated.

Taos had long been a byword for potent alcohol, and evidence points to use of harder stuff. Despite seeing a friend institutionalized after a bad peyote trip, Mabel Luhan had taken peyote at least once with her friends from the pueblo. As some of the hippies befriended the Pueblo people, they, too, were invited to join in the peyote ceremonies.

New Mexicans had long cultivated their own smoking product: a noxious, tobacco-like weed. They called it *punche*—or *mota* in Taos—and both men and women smoked it voraciously. Smokers carried little bags of trimmed cornhusks and punche (or mota) with which they deftly rolled neat, but smelly, little cigarettes. While the fine folk of Chihuahua scorned this

Playing at the fandango. Jane Abrams print of a carving used repeatedly in *El Crepúsculo*, 1930–38. *CSWR.*

practice, the punche trade was brisk at the trade fairs. Although the sale of punche was strictly against Spanish law, as contrary to the king's monopoly, no official would dream of enforcing the law. Various governors considered regulation and taxation, but only Governor Albino Perez, tragically and disastrously, tried it.

Whatever it was the hippies saw growing in local fields, they thought it was marijuana and took it as an invitation to grow their own. Every commune but the Lama Foundation was growing on some scale. The Lama Foundation strictly prohibited drug use (which many attribute to its continued existence today), but members of the other communes eagerly consumed whatever drugs were available.

Hacienda courtyards, which used to bustle with industrious homesteader families, now seethed with "gyrating, flowing…dancing freaks" as LSD-spiked electric punch flowed at parties. The Hog Farm's "hallucination-extended family" welcomed Ken Kesey's Merry Pranksters for some particularly memorable parties, including acid-impaired bus races on state highways. Although the bus races ended in laughs rather than tears, many youth overdosed, freaked out or contracted the hepatitis that ran rampant through the communes.

Busloads of hippies would park near the local attractions, like the Ponce de Leon or Manby Hot Springs or the Taos Gorge, and get wild. Sometimes local kids would wade in with baseball bats, but increasingly, the local kids would join them. That worried parents, who feared the radical youth culture. Indeed, marijuana and hallucinogens were only the tip of the iceberg. Cocaine, pills and heroin were also flowing into the valley.

Before long, a growing Texas biker gang took control of the narcotics traffic. The Bandidos Motorcycle Club claimed, "We are the people our parents warned us about" and "Expect no mercy." Despite these warnings, many communes welcomed them and the drugs they bought. The bikers joined the parties at the hot springs, adding heavy drinking, the maddening noise of their chopped bikes and public pot smoking to the mix of nudity and general freakishness.

"Oh, Lookat!" Tourists have long enjoyed the casual pandemonium of Taos. Jane Abrams print of a carving by Ward Lockwood for *Laughing Horse* 18 (September 1930). *CSWR.*

At first, residents approached the hippies politely to make their biker friends leave. But many young people depended on the steady flow of substances that offered such an interesting alternative to fencing pastures. Conflicts escalated with the locals. Bandidos and locals soon exchanged shots.

A biker named Mongol, or Funky James, was staying at New Buffalo before the shootout that killed him. Two bikers died in a hail of bullets up at Ojo Sarco. One biker named Lobo killed two locals, brothers from an old family, before turning his gun on himself. The legendary outlaw biker Chief Joseph engaged narcotics agents in Santa Fe in a gun battle, endangering bystanders in pursuit of his Wild West fantasy. The Bandidos nursed their grudges for a long time, and many shootouts were initiated in revenge for some previous wrong. A dwarf, a beautiful but vicious woman and the powder keg of rancor that characterized the early 1970s sparked a catastrophic gun battle at Arroyo Hondo's Gay Nineties cantina.

In addition to the criminal activity, the buses full of hippies and the cavalcade of Bandidos created more mundane but equally serious problems. With so many Taos residents enjoying endless leisure time and endless parties, the most lovely and popular natural areas started to get trashed with bottles, cigarette butts, needles and other detritus. The hot springs became particularly contested, and finally, Taos Pueblo stepped in.

Although Ponce de Leon was on private land, the pueblo asserted right of ancestral use. As one war chief said, "Blue Lake, the Río Grande, Red Clay, the Hot Springs—these areas are critical to our well-being. Without them, we would not exist." Heartened by the success with Blue Lake, the elders decided to start taking back the hot springs. Surprisingly, the political alliance the hippies forged with the pueblo over Blue Lake extended to this effort. Comprised of Hispaños, pueblo members and Anglos, the Taos Land Trust worked steadily for three decades to preserve critical lands and waters in the valley.

WAR IS OVER! IF YOU WANT IT

By 1973, the wilder hippies had drifted off in search of more happening scenes, and those who stayed were those with the will to work hard digging ditches, fencing fields, tending animals and building bridges with the old-timers. Shared hard work was a language the Taos understood, so the remaining hippies slowly became important members of the community. Just as Taos slowly but successfully assimilated Plains culture, Hispanic culture and the culture of high art and intellect, so has hippie culture become part of the fabric of Taos society.

Even Dennis Hopper became a sober, model citizen eventually. In 2009, Hopper became the honorary mayor of Taos. His single run-in with the

Wavy Gravy and Jahanara Romney, 2013. *Courtesy Paul G. Green via Creative Commons.*

Taos authorities happened in 1975, when he was arrested, booked and released on charges of reckless driving, leaving the scene of an accident and evading arrest. Wavy Gravy and his wife, Jahanara Romney (formerly the Hog Farm's police commissioner), eventually shut down New Mexico's Hog Farm and concentrated their operations in California. Today, they also operate a circus and performing arts camp for children near the remaining Hog Farm. Others, like the eminent author John Nichols, make an effort to remain a thorn in the side of authority.

Even the police mellowed in their attitude toward the stoned longhairs. One "very mellow" raid on New Buffalo in the spring of 1972 involved nine squad cars with over twenty officers. With breaks for coffee and snacks provided by the kindly women of the commune, the police searched the commune and easily found the marijuana-growing area. One man asked the police if they had to give up all their lovingly tended plants. The narc considered. "Just give them the big ones," he finally decided.

Everyone was happy that day. The police had something to show for their work; the hippies lost only about half the plants, and their precious hash supply was undisturbed. As the police pulled away, a flood of hippies who had been hiding down by the river returned to the commune with the rest of the drugs.

Another raid on New Buffalo over a year later came in search of a man suspected of plotting to assassinate Nixon. Believing him to be in the Taos area, police had launched a massive manhunt to bring him to justice. Helicopters and police swarmed down on New Buffalo, but when residents politely asked the officers to return their guns to the patrol cars, they complied without a murmur.

The Bureau of Land Management started managing Manby Hot Springs, and today's residents work together to keep it clean and peaceful (although nudity never went out of style). The Taos Land Trust finally signed the land holding the Ponce de Leon springs over to Taos Pueblo in July 2012. War chief Benito Sandoval spoke at the transfer ceremony: "It is important to preserve these areas for the future of our children and all who live here. We are very grateful."

RECOMMENDED READING

Bodine, John J. "The Taos Blue Lake Ceremony." *American Indian Quarterly* 12, no. 2 (Spring 1988).

———. "Taos Blue Lake Controversy." *Journal of Ethnic Studies* 6, no. 1 (Spring 1978).

Bullis, Don. *New Mexico & Politicians of the Past.* Los Ranchos de Albuquerque, NM: Rio Grande Books, 2009.

Chávez, Thomas E. *Conflict and Acculturation: Manuel Alvarez's 1842 Memorial.* Santa Fe: Museum of New Mexico Press, 1989.

Curtis, Edward S. *The North American Indian: Being a Series of Volumes Picturing and Describing the Indians of the United States, and Alaska.* Vol. 16, *The Tiwa, The Keres.* Cambridge, MA: University Press, 1926.

De Huff, Elizabeth W. *Traditional Pueblo Indian Tales.* New York: Harcourt, Brace and Company, 1922.

Espinosa, Aurelio M. *The Folklore of Spain in the American Southwest: Traditional Spanish Folk Literature in Northern New Mexico and Southern Colorado.* Norman: University of Oklahoma Press, 1990.

Espinosa, Jose M. "Spanish Folk-Tales from New Mexico." In *Memoirs of the American Folklore Society.* New York: J.J. Augustin, 1937.

Galbraith, Den. *Turbulent Taos.* Santa Fe, NM: Sunstone Press, 2011.

Garrard, Lewis H. *Wah-To-Yah and the Taos Trail: Or, Prairie Travel and Scalp Dances, with a Look at Los Rancheros from Muleback and the Rocky Mountain Camp-fire.* Cincinnati, OH: H.W. Derby & Company, 1850.

Gordon-McCutchan, R.C. *The Taos Indians and the Battle for Blue Lake*. Santa Fe, NM: Red Crane Books, 1991.

Hemp, Bill. *Taos: Landmarks and Legends*. Boulder: University Press of Colorado, 2002.

Hignett, Sean. *Brett, from Bloomsbury to New Mexico: A Biography*. London: Hodder and Stoughton, 1985.

Hodge, Frederick W., George P. Hammond and Agapito Rey. *Benavides' Revised Memorial of 1634*. Albuquerque: University of New Mexico Press, 1945.

Hollenbach, Margaret. *Lost and Found: My Life in a Group Marriage Commune*. Albuquerque: University of New Mexico Press, 2004.

Jenkens, Myra E. "Taos Pueblo and Its Neighbors." *New Mexico Historical Review* 42, no. 2 (1966).

Keltz, Iris and Ed Sanders. *Scrapbook of a Taos Hippie: Tribal Tales from the Heart of a Cultural Revolution*. El Paso, TX: Cinco Puntos Press, 2000.

Kessell, John L., Rick Hendricks and Meredith Dodge. *Blood on the Boulders: The Journals of Don Diego de Vargas, 1694–1697*. Albuquerque: University of New Mexico Press, 1988.

Kopecky, Arthur. *Leaving New Buffalo*. Albuquerque: University of New Mexico Press, 2006.

Kopecky, Arthur, and Peter Coyote. *New Buffalo: Journals from a Taos Commune*. Albuquerque: University of New Mexico Press, 2004.

Lacy, Ann, and Anne Valley-Fox. *Outlaws and Desperados: A New Mexico Federal Writers' Project Book*. Santa Fe, NM: Sunstone Press, 2008.

Law, Lisa. *Flashing on the Sixties*. Oxford, MS: Squarebooks, 2000.

Lawrence D.H. *Women in Love*. New York: Viking Compass, 1970.

Luhan, Mabel D. *Intimate Memories: The Autobiography of Mabel Dodge Luhan*. Edited by Lois P. Rudnick. Santa Fe, NM: Sunstone Press, 1999.

McNierney, Michael. *Taos 1847: The Revolt in Contemporary Accounts*. Boulder, CO: Johnson Publishing Company, 1980.

Opler, Morris E. "Myths and Tales of the Jicarilla Apache Indians." In *Memoirs of the American Folklore Society*. No. 31. New York: J. Augustin, 1938.

Parsons, Elsie C. *Taos Tales*. The American Folk-Lore Society. New York: J.J. Augustin, 1940.

Peters, James S. *Headless in Taos: The Dark Fated Tale of Arthur Rochford Manby*. Santa Fe, NM: Sunstone Press, 2012.

Roberts, David. *The Pueblo Revolt: The Secret Rebellion That Drove the Spaniards Out of the Southwest*. New York: Simon and Schuster, 2008.

Rosenbaum, Robert J. *Mexicano Resistance in the Southwest*. Austin: University of Texas Press, 1981.

Rudnick, Lois P. *The Suppressed Memoirs of Mabel Dodge Luhan: Sex, Syphilis, and Psychoanalysis in the Making of Modern American Culture*. Albuquerque: University of New Mexico Press, 2012.

———. *Utopian Vistas: The Mabel Dodge Luhan House and the American Counterculture*. Albuquerque: University of New Mexico Press, 1996.

Sanchez, George I. *Forgotten People: A Study of New Mexico*. Albuquerque, NM: Horn and Wallace, 1967.

Scholes, France V. "Church and State in New Mexico, 1610–1650." *New Mexico Historical Review* 11 (1936).

Sherman, John. *Taos: A Pictorial History*. Santa Fe, NM: William Gannon, 1990.

Simmons, Marc. *Spanish Government in New Mexico*. Albuquerque: University of New Mexico Press, 1968.

Squires, Michael. *D.H. Lawrence and Frieda: A Portrait of Love and Loyalty*. London: Andre Deutsch, 2008.

Thomas, Alfred B. *Forgotten Frontiers: A Study of the Spanish Indian Policy of Don Juan Bautista de Anza Governor of New Mexico, 1777–1787*. Norman: University of Oklahoma Press, 1932.

Twitchell, Ralph E. *The Spanish Archives of New Mexico*. Vol. 2. Cedar Rapids, IA: Torch Press, 1914.

Weber, David J. *On the Edge of Empire. The Taos Hacienda of los Martinez*. Santa Fe: Museum of New Mexico Press, 1996.

———. *The Taos Trappers: The Fur Trade in the Far Southwest, 1540–1846*. Norman: University of Oklahoma Press, 1980.

Zumwalt, Rosemary L. *Wealth and Rebellion: Elsie Clewes Parsons, Anthropologist and Folklorist*. Urbana: University of Illinois Press, 1992.

ABOUT THE AUTHOR

Ellen Dornan loves learning about the rich heritage of the American West, particularly the scoundrels, misfits and visionaries who make history so interesting. In commemoration of New Mexico's centennial of statehood, Ms. Dornan wrote *Forgotten Tales of New Mexico*, and as a cultural resources interpreter specializing in new media, she developed the online Centennial Atlas of Historic New Mexico Maps (atlas.nmhum.org).